RADICAL
RAGS

FASHIONS OF THE SIXTIES

By Joel Lobenthal

Abbeville Press

Publishers

New York

EDITOR: Alan Axelrod

DESIGNER: Renée Khatami

PRODUCTION SUPERVISOR: Hope Koturo

First edition
Published in the United States of America by Abbeville
Press, Inc.

Library of Congress Cataloging-in-Publication Data

Lobenthal, Joel.
  Radical rags : fashions of the Sixties / by Joel
Lobenthal.
    p. cm.
  Includes bibliographical references.
  ISBN 0-89659-930-2
  1. Fashion—History—20th Century. 2.
Costume—History—20th century. I. Title.
GT596.L64   1990
391'.009'046—dc20   89-29854
                                              CIP

FRONT COVER: *Lauren Hutton in Betsey Johnson's slip dress of soft plastic with do-it-yourself stick-ons of sequin sheeting material, spring 1966; vinyl shoes by Herbert Levine*

BACK COVER: *Peggy Moffitt in a Cardin sequinned couture evening dress, 1966*

HALF-TITLE PAGE: *Courrèges trouser suit from his spring 1965 couture collection*

FRONTISPIECE: *The World discotheque, New York, 1966*

PAGES 4–5: *Richard Avedon portrait of Benedetta Barzini, New York, May 1966*

CONTENTS

LONDON

"Fashion allows you to be what you want. You can dress the part and—my God, it happens!" It is December 1988, and Mary Quant is talking in the conference room of her London headquarters, hub of an international empire. A few blocks away, in Chelsea's King's Road, Quant first set up shop in 1955. It was a space not much larger than the room in which she now sits. Quant's Bazaar boutique came to be regarded as the opening shot in the fashion revolution begun in London and spread to the rest of the Western world during the 1960s.

"Fashion is a very renewing force—a way of not getting bored with oneself. It lets you then look out on everyone else, because you're not so preoccupied within yourself." Quant won her spurs by an attempt to make the self-actualization afforded by fashion available to a wider audience than had shared in its dividends during her youth. In 1955, the Paris couturier was still an oracle. Wealthy Englishwomen patronized the French couturiers or their British counterparts—the London "top twelve." Increasingly pallid and poorly made couture derivations were available to each descending economic echelon. "What was wrong at that stage was that fashion only came through one route," Quant recalls, "which designed for a way of life which was very much that of a minority. I came in wanting to create for people like me and for a life that was very real: women who had a job and a fantasy life that took that job into account."

Bazaar opened at a propitious moment. After the privations of the immediate postwar years, Britain was savoring a new abundance of consumer goods—summed up by Prime Minister Harold Macmillan's catch phrase, "You've never had it so good." With the construction of the socialist state, it also appeared that the fruits of British prosperity would be distributed more equitably than ever before. Following on this apparent abolition of class stratification came a wholesale questioning of venerable British institutions and Conventional Wisdom. In 1966, Jocelyn Stevens, publisher of *Queen*, recalled the exuberant and optimistic unbuttoning of Britain in the late '50s: "all sort of completely accepted attitudes were proven wrong . . . we lashed out at everything with a vengeance. All the household gods were attacked, all the accepted attitudes. It was the most marvelous time to start everything."

Quant was born in 1934, the daughter of two Welsh schoolteachers, who "had what was then quite a rare point of view: that it was important a girl had a career." They were not thrilled about her choice of vocation, however, believing that "fashion was a very dangerous sort of business." Her parents were not inhibiting, but they were concerned—"Strongly!" Quant laughs today. At Goldsmith's College of Art in London, where Quant compromised with her parents by pursuing a diploma in art education, she met Alexander Plunket Greene, who would become her husband and business partner. Plunket Greene was descended from a clan of

Mother and daughter bias-cut crêpe dresses designed by Barbara Hulanicki for Biba in 1969

flamboyant libertines upon whom Evelyn Waugh had modeled several of his blue-blooded protagonists. Quant and Plunket Greene's alliance would epitomize a contemporary fusion of two diametrically opposed British classes: blue-blood aesthete and cautious bourgeois. Impious but level-headed, Quant's quiet conviction was a foil to Plunket Greene's colorful bravado, and a refreshing contrast to the florid pronouncements of many French couturiers. Discussing her role in the '60s millennium, Quant once stated: "No designer is ever responsible for such a revolution. . . . I just happened to start when that 'something in the air' was coming to a boil."

In 1974, Plunket Greene recalled: "When we started, we were really so bloody lonely. We thought our parents' generation was mad, but thought we were the only ones to feel like this. We seemed alone. Then we realized that a whole lot of young people felt the same way." After leaving school, Quant apprenticed with a custom milliner in Mayfair while she and Plunket Greene fell in with a a band of renegade artists and dilettantes who congregated in London's Chelsea district, the seat of that city's bohemian life since the beginning of the century. At the head of King's Road in Chelsea's Sloane Square stands the Royal Court Theatre, where John Osborne's *Look Back in Anger* was launching a school of protest drama analyzing the life of the British working class. Outside the theater assembled London's beatnik tribe, regular

Mary Quant, 1988

(OPPOSITE, TOP) Mary Quant and Alexander Plunket Greene, her husband and business partner: "I wanted everyone to retain the grace of a child and not have to become stilted, confined, ugly beings," Quant said. "So I created clothes that . . . allowed people to run, to jump, to leap, to retain their precious freedom."

(OPPOSITE, BOTTOM) Mary Quant, thirty-two in 1966, was invested with the Order of the British Empire and wrote a best-selling autobiography.

patrons of the espresso bars that had begun to open along King's Road. Ernestine Carter of the London *Times* recalled the "long-haired, bearded young men in skinny pants and leather jackets and longer haired . . . young women in short tight skirts and black stockings or high black boots, under what looked like out-grown coats that were more mouse than mink."

"I wanted to express that feeling," Quant said. She left her millinery salon and opened Bazaar together with Plunket Greene and Archie McNair, a lawyer who had spearheaded one of the first coffee bars on King's Road. When Quant could not readily find the type of clothes she wanted at wholesale, she began filling Bazaar with her own designs. The clothes she offered were less stringent than couture orthodoxy but quirkier than most mass-produced fare. She took direction both from the beatnik zeitgeist permeating Chelsea as well as the residual memory of her childhood dance classes. Peering into tap dancing classes from the threshold of the ballroom class in which she was enrolled, Quant enviously glimpsed the tap students' black tights and black patent-leather shoes. "It stuck in my mind," she recalls. The inevitable result of these influences was the steadily rising hemline that would one day earn Quant the accolade "mother of the miniskirt."

The King's Road itself, destined to become London's most spectacular shopping artery in the '60s, was in the 1950s a cozy thoroughfare lined with family-owned stores. Bazaar made a kink in the street's placidity. Quant and Plunket Greene coined droll names for their designs, like "Hook, line, and sinker" and "Lock, stock, and barrel" for three-piece outfits, "Booby traps" for a bra. Together with display designer John Bates, they orchestrated humorous, arresting window displays that stopped pedestrians in their tracks.

In *Quant by Quant*, published in 1966, the designer writes of her childhood dread of adulthood, of the horror aroused by the brindled pompadours and stiletto heels that were considered women's birthright during the '40s. To Quant and her generation, the overblown femininity of the '40s and early '50s was oppressive both decoratively and symbolically; she and her contemporaries upended the sanctions that these appurtenances imposed and crystallized. "Growing up was a debilitating thing as presented to one," she recalls today. "It meant that you couldn't do this or that, rather than, as it might seem now, you *can* do this and that." At the time Bazaar debuted, "fashion wasn't designed for young people," Quant notes. The traditional progression of English women's dress was from starched school uniform to dour suits and evening gowns. Quant's Bazaar augured the revival of the very young woman as a fashion leader, after nearly thirty years in eclipse. While the Paris couture deified soignée maturity, the English rebels of the '60s elevated the unmarried demoiselle to the most influential platform she would command during the century. The dominant prototype in fashion for

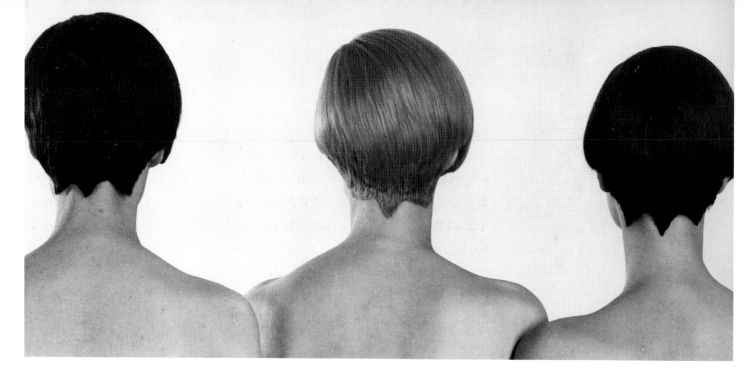

12

the first half of the '60s was a free-spirited sprite, often artistic and eccentric—a "kook." Kicking up her heels, she freely exercised the liberties of youth rather than observing maturity's imperative that composure be maintained at all costs. In 1967 Maureen Cleave in the *New York Times Magazine* limned the philosophy informing Quant's work: "the young should look like the young. . . . The old could, if they wished, look like the young, but the young must not on any account look like the old."

Quant's clothes expressed the "jubilation" resulting from women's newly fluid status, a turn away from the obligatory yokes of husband and family insisted upon during the postwar reconstruction. Quant explains: "Women had been building to this for a long time, but before the pill there couldn't really be a true emancipation. It's very clear in the look, in the exuberance of the time—a rather childlike exhilaration: 'Wow—look at me!—isn't it lovely? At last, at last!'"

With her gamine's bob and knee-baring skirts draped on her softly rounded figure, Quant herself was an eloquent model of her own designs. "My clothes and my look are like an exaggeration of myself—only more so, a sort of caricature," she said in 1963. "I love Coco Chanel and Marlene Dietrich, people who exaggerate themselves." "Good taste is death, vulgarity is life," Quant proclaimed. Bazaar was a broadside against the staid reserve of traditional British dressing. Quant's solecisms extended to her embrace of synthetic materials. At the height of her influence, she complained that many people were unable to understand "what a machine is capable of doing *itself* instead of making it copy what the hand does." Machine-made textiles appealed to her as a liberation from the manacled laboriousness of hand work. "Machine-made things can, of course, look just churned out," Quant professes today, "or they can look like a delicious soufflé that happened with a pure kind of joy—without anybody's tears on them."

Neither Quant, Plunket Greene, nor McNair possessed prior experience in clothing manufacture. The store's galloping success was due to the freshness of their viewpoint; yet their innocence made Bazaar's first years a trial by fire for its principals. Quant realized that her store's notoriety had extended beyond its local impact when American manufacturers began making purchases, "saying, in that charming way Americans will, 'What I'm going to do is manufacture this in mass quantities.' In my stupidity I thought that was rather monstrous. It took me a bit of time to realize that was the only real applause, for God's sake." Paul Young, envoy from J. C. Penney, requested that she design four annual collections for the American chain. "He just stood us on our heads: We didn't know how to produce these *fantastic* quantities. It's another lovely American characteristic not to accept 'No.' 'Yes, of course you can do it!' they told us. So we tried, with all sorts of consequences, but we did try! What we were doing here had anticipated something that was international. It was quite a shock—quite an exciting shock!''

For diligent and intelligent Britishers of every stratum, art schools were a ladder to success in postwar England. Generous government subsidies made it possible for an unprecedented number of students of humble economic origin to pursue careers in the fine and commercial arts. At the Royal College of Art, a graduate fashion department had been inaugurated in the late 1940s by former *Vogue* editor-in-chief Madge Garland, who brought the program into the fashion forefront during the first half of the '50s. Her successor was Professor Janey Ironside, godmother to a posse of bright young designers who rose precipitately during the '60s. "I wish I were young now," Professor Ironside confessed in 1968. "My youth was spent in dreary clothes that one wore because one had to."

Foale and Tuffin's keyhole lace dress was a classic of the early '60s.

Professor Ironside "was a very free spirit," recalls Sally Tuffin, one of the RCA's most celebrated alumni. "I remember when I went for my interview, she said 'Do you like shoes?' 'Well, I *love* buying shoes,' was my reply. It was totally the wrong one. I should have been much more serious. But she wanted that spontaneity."

The design partnership of Sally Tuffin and Marion Foale became a standard-bearer for the Royal College of Art's fashion wing. Foale and Tuffin's celebrity during the '60s broadcast the expanded opportunities available to talented and accredited youth. The design team broke with tradition by forsaking a long apprenticeship with an established firm. They succeeded in establishing their own business soon after graduation. "We were dressing ourselves and our friends, and it just happened to be the sort of things that people wanted," Sally Tuffin modestly recalls today. Tuffin currently runs a pottery business with her husband. As students, "we were trained to see, to explore, to enjoy ourselves. We felt as though we could go off and do anything, without restriction. We didn't feel that we had to prove ourselves by buying a smart car and a Filofax. Young people have got such enthusiasm; it's very sad that today they're made to feel stuck into a groove before they begin."

Born in 1938, Tuffin, the daughter of a printer and a dressmaker, attests that in England during the '50s, "there weren't clothes for young people at all—one just looked like one's

Susannah York in Foale and Tuffin's linen trouser suit and an organza Trilby hat created by James Wedge for the film Kaleidoscope

mother." Imported American culture, however, supplied more sympathetic role models. Tuffin recalls experimenting with "fuller skirts and little cardigans and pony tails. We saw them in James Dean films and made them ourselves. But no jeans or trousers as yet."

Marion Foale's father was a menswear manufacturer's agent, but Foale, also born in 1938, became interested in fashion design only while attending the Walthomstow art school, where Tuffin was also a student. Later, at the Royal College, the two were encouraged by a lecture on costing given by Mary Quant and Alexander Plunket Greene. "They said they didn't follow hard and fast rules about pricing a garment. They had a very light-hearted attitude towards it, which was wonderful. We realized, *then*, that we probably could do what they were—we didn't have to go and work for another firm."

Following their certification in 1960, Foale and Tuffin nevertheless did attempt to interest established manufacturers in their designs. "I distinctly remember one of them saying: 'Take my advice, go and get married,'" Tuffin recalls. "That was the *last* thing on our minds. You don't train for seven years to go and get married, do you? They weren't telling us: 'We don't

16

like what you do.' Indeed, a couple of the designs we showed them did mysteriously turn up in the stores next season! They probably thought we were immature. We didn't look very adult. We didn't try to."

Milliner James Wedge, an RCA classmate, led them to showroom premises adjacent to his near Carnaby Street, a West End alley that would metamorphosize into a hotbed of trendy men's boutiques. At the time, however, it was "just like a little suburban street," replete with pipe shop, dry cleaners, grocers, and shoe repair shop. Beginning with one floor, Foale and Tuffin would eventually take over two Regency houses. "But it wasn't a question of 'setting up in business,'" Tuffin insists. "We had no overhead. Our rent was six pounds a week. So it was relatively easy: if you had the energy and the ideas you could just do it."

Foale and Tuffin's work found its first major showcase at Wooland's, a large department store that was "one of the first big shops doing anything with a young feeling," Foale remembers. Buyer Vanessa Denza purchased their designs for Wooland's "21 Shop," which had opened in 1961. Top model Jean Shrimpton appeared in *Vogue*'s "Young Idea" pages (edited then by the late Claire Rendelsham), wearing a Foale and Tuffin, and "We were on our way." They had been in business but a year when *Queen*'s Caterine Milinaire and Marit Allen observed that "they have immediately cut out a very clear and bright image for themselves. Their ideas are young, simple, wearable, more than with it—often before it."

Tuffin and Foale's pantsuits were the mother lode of trouser suits in the '60s. "The cut was incredible, the best I've ever seen. I'm sure Saint Laurent was influenced by them," designer Betsey Johnson avows. Tuffin remembers how outré trousers for women appeared, even to the designers themselves. "When we first cut pants, instead of a skirt, with the jacket, we actually fell about laughing." Tuffin describes the suit's configuration as "slim sleeves, no shoulders, straight lines, quite fitted, in the manner of a riding jacket way, but really soft. Heavy tailoring just wasn't 'on.'" Their trousers were hipsters: "There was no waist—no waist at *all* in the '60s," Tuffin recalls. "Our clothes *had* to be comfortable," she says. "That was the main requirement."

In August 1964, Foale, wearing a stone-cut velvet dress trimmed in pink velvet, and Tuffin, dressed in an eggplant-and-gold print suit, received *WWD* in their petite Carnaby Street showroom. Pop music roared, a "man wall" displayed pin-ups of the Beatles and other current idols, and the designers dodged "phones ringing, buyers dashing in and out, frantic calls for more beige corduroy trouser suits." Warhol Superstar "Baby" Jane Holzer "was tearing the racks apart" the day the journal's Ann Ryan visited the young design team. "This stuff swings. . . . It's much better than New York," Holzer carolled to the newspaper's reporter. She jumped "in and out of pantsuits, clean crêpe dresses cut like cycler's shirts, or ferociously banded in rugby stripes—purple and jade—and the new Foale and Tuffin Pop Art prints."

The following year, the two designers unveiled a retail operation adjacent to their wholesale headquarters. Their clothes were now available at department stores across England and at the cutting edge Countdown boutique on King's Road. By then, Tuffin and Foale "were really influencing the rest of the world," recalls Zandra Rhodes, who made a beeline to the two designers with her own first wholesale fabric designs. In 1965, Foale and Tuffin were among the debut resources stocked by Manhattan's seminal "Paraphernalia" shop, where, Betsey Johnson recalls, "Their pantsuits sold like hotcakes." That year, the two young partners traveled to American to join a promotional tour stumping Paraphernalia and its wholesale arm, Youthquake. In the U.S. they were bemused by department store buyers slumming in Mod attire. At a runway show in a large suburban department store, they encountered buyers "all wearing our clothes or similar editions. We thought, 'Gosh, they're really quite hip.' But after the show they all changed back into their own clothes. They knew our work was commercially viable, but they didn't wear it. Fair enough, but at the time we were so dismayed!"

Garnished with hand finishing and often fashioned from pure silk, Foale and Tuffin's clothes sold for between approximately $20.00 and $40.00. While not inaccessible, their work was a significant, if indispensable, strain on junior British purses of the '60s. Yet their aesthetic was decidedly demotic: "We can't stand deb models," Foale told the *Daily Express*. "We have deb customers, but that's enough debbery," Tuffin added. "It was very much street culture that influenced us," Tuffin explains today. Foale, who currently runs a knitwear business, explains: "When we were students, it was all Paris—Balenciaga, the real Dior, Givenchy. We were really into it, but as soon as we left college, we thought all that was for someone else altogether—an older woman who was very rich—and it seemed rather boring, perhaps. We were young—we wanted something for *us* that was not too expensive, that we could go to discotheques and have fun in."

In England, men's underwear briefs are known as "Y-fronts" in reference to the particular way that the fly opening is folded. Punning on this hearty staple of men's apparel, Tuffin and Foale splashed giant Y's across the countenance of a group of shift dresses. "I suppose that sums up the '60s!" Tuffin laughs.

For British working-class youth of the '60s, clothes and popular music were the nuclei around which a self-contained culture coalesced. The appellation "Mod" referred originally to a group of scooter-riding, clothes-obsessed young men, but the term was soon used generically to

The minimal dress of '60s Mod was accompanied by oversize jewelry and eye-popping accessories.

(Opposite) London teenager Jane Gozzett ran an after-school business supplying '30s-style knitted caps to Biba.

denote many pockets of youth whose appearance broadcast their independence. Guiding *WWD* readers through London's Mod subculture in August 1964, columnist Carol Bjorkman discovered that among this exotic race, "names we have come to associate with the height of fashion they ignore." Twiggy recalled in her autobiography: "The great point about those clothes we wore was that we had to make the things ourselves, because they were never in fashion long enough for the fashion people to catch up." Yet at London's Biba boutique, working class youth found a clothes store that could keep pace with their restless sartorial experimentation—a store that would, in fact, become a second home.

"To all optimists, fatalists, and dreamers" Barbara Hulanicki, Biba's founder, dedicated her 1983 memoirs. Today, Hulanicki admits that in so doing she was penning an homage to the like-minded; Hulanicki is an inveterate romantic. The couture purveyed dreams that tantalized by their exclusivity; their appeal to the general public hinged on the delicious melancholy of unfulfilled desire. Inspired by celluloid fantasies, however, Hulanicki created in Biba a dream palace that turned no one away. Biba's chatelaine passionately believed in the right of all to realize their aspirations. Biba's prices were legendary. "The poorest student could afford to say 'I'll have it' before asking 'How much?'" Georgina Howell noted in the 1975 anthology *In Vogue*. During London in the 1960s, "it was a terrible shame to show you were making money, or seeming to exploit people," Hulanicki explains. "The criterion was *not* to have fabulous ledgers. There were only a few designers who were very together. We practically gave our things away to the public."

Hulanicki was born in 1936 and raised in Palestine, where her father was Polish consul general; shortly after World War II, however, he was assassinated by a terrorist cabal. She immigrated to England with her aunt, her mother, and her two sisters. "I was amazed at how free the English of my age were to do what they wanted," she recalls. Compared to the extended network of traditional Middle European culture, "there's very little family cohesion, except in the upper classes," she claims. "That's why England's been so strong with creativity—it comes from the worker's families, and the first thing the kids do is go out on their own. Their talent is very crude and unaffected by tradition, so it's marvelously free. However, the process isn't working at the moment, because the generation that's coming up now isn't being educated."

Hulanicki's adolescence was dominated by her dowager Aunt Sophie, her mother's older sister, who was among "the last of that kind of women whose whole ploy was to titillate, to keep a man on a string until he was screaming to have you. That's how you acquired your diamonds—because once you got down to business, your market value diminished." Despite,

or because of, the intricate choreography of ensnarement in which her aunt had been trained, it was she "who always impressed upon me that I must be independent."

Never imagining how violently her generation would reject them, the adolescent Hulanicki was prey to the ruling ideals of beauty. "When I was sixteen," she recalls, "my dream was to wear a black dress and pearls and have my hair in this great dark chignon in order to look thirty." After studying at an art college, she began in the late '50s to work as a fashion illustrator. Close-up exposure to couture dimmed some of its luster in her eyes. The house of Balenciaga typified "the snobbery that was designed to make everyone feel inferior. The shows weren't there to be enjoyed. They were all about making you desire something you couldn't have—or didn't have at that moment. If you walked in wearing a dress from another couture house you were still second-class. They probably were especially haughty then because they

Moving day for Biba, February 1966; leading the charge are pop singer Cilla Black and television hostess Cathy McGowan.

could feel it was all about to come to an end." The young professional further objected to couture's explicit elucidation of the economic dependence of its customer, at odds with Hulanicki's own hard-won independence: "The couture was for kept women," she declares unequivocally.

She soon realized the dearth of well-designed and accessibly priced attire in her adopted land. "At that time, the manufacturers in England didn't understand cutting. That's why they used drawings so frequently. I was forever sketching clothes that looked nice on paper but in reality were awful. The sleeve was set into the garment without allowing for any movement: every time you shifted your arm the whole garment lifted." Driving down King's Road one day, Hulanicki was galvanized by the sight of dresses pinned to panels in the windows of Kiki Byrne's newly opened boutique. "I thought the door had opened on a new world," she rhap-

When Biba opened a satellite branch in New York's Bergdorf Goodman, the windows of the specialty store featured Biba's trademark artifacts.

Biba's mother and daughter panne velvet dresses, designed for Biba in 1969 by owner Barbara Hulanicki

sodizes. Byrne made ''these wonderful black dresses—not the staid old ones I wanted when I was sixteen, but shifts that weren't over-designed.'' After working for Quant, Byrne had opened her own boutique, Glass & Black. ''Kiki was a real street dresser,'' Hulanicki remembers.''I saw her twisting at the Saddle Room one night early in the '60s. She looked so amazing. She was wearing a tight little black mini and a slim, black cropped top with very long narrow sleeves cuffed in black marabou.''

After marrying Stephen Fitz-Simon, a young advertising account executive, Hulanicki and her husband looked for a business venture that would synchronize their energies. They decided to open ''Biba's Postal Boutique,'' a mail order clothing service that took its title from the diminutive form of Hulanicki's sister's name, Biruta. After Hulanicki's sleeveless gingham shift was featured in Felicity Green's *Daily Mirror* column, Biba was snowed under with orders. Their clothes garnered valuable visibility, too, when Hulanicki started to design for Cathy McGowan, the impeccably chic ''Queen of the Mods,'' hostess of the popular music television show ''Ready, Steady, Go.''

By 1964, when Hulanicki opened the first Biba emporium, she was ''*the* name in the lives of Britain's fashion-hungry, fiercely individualistic Mods,'' *WWD* reported. Biba opened in a former drugstore on Abingdon Road, away from any of London's major shopping corridors. ''We avoided Chelsea and Knightsbridge and all the obvious places because we didn't want to be associated with any existing look,'' Hulanicki explained soon after cutting the ribbon on her new retail home.

She staffed her premises with a battalion of self-sufficient, single, often very young Londoners, a breed ''incredibly bright, quick and resilient. They were earning their own money; they weren't living at home anymore. When they went out they paid for themselves.'' They hailed from diverse backgrounds, but unilaterally subscribed to the particular disdain '60s youth evinced for those over twenty-five. ''I'll always remember them coming to me once. ''We've just caught a shoplifter. She's really old—quite a middle-aged woman.' '*Really?*' I asked. 'What age is she?' 'She's twenty-seven,' they told me.''

''One Saturday, Marcello Mastroianni came in,'' Hulanicki adds. ''He was at his height, and of course I was passing out. But all the girls said, 'Oh, he's such an old man.' They wouldn't have anything to do with him!''

The narrow elongation of Biba's taproot silhouette highlighted ''the tiny little bones,'' of a teenaged population weaned on austerity rations. ''That generation was minute,'' Hulanicki remembers. ''The average shoe size then was 3½ or 4. When we came back to London in the '80s it had jumped to 5½. When we opened a department at Bergdorf Goodman [in 1970], we brought our boots, but no American woman could put them on. Their muscles were so much better developed."

"I love old things," Hulanicki said in 1966. "Modern things are so cold. I need things that have lived." She established the blueprint for her successive Bibas by retaining the original fittings in the Abingdon Road shop. The first Biba was small, but boasted lofty ceilings. "I always liked very grand settings," Hulanicki relates. Antique embossed-leather screens were used to corral a communal changing area in lieu of traditionally demarcated booths. Dresses were displayed on antique coat racks: three or four per crook, surmounted by matching hats on the uppermost rungs. Jewelry was spread out over a mahogany vanity table fit for the dressing room of a nineteenth-century ballerina. Dark walnut wainscoting and the sparkle of brass finishes evoked Victorian spit and polish; etched glass was imprinted with the BIBA logo in Celtic lettering of black and gold. Biba was uniquely enticing. Georgina Howell recalls the "jumbled clothes, feathers, beads and Lurex spilling out over the counters like treasure in a cave." Over the years, the store moved to successively larger premises: to Kensington Church Street in 1966, Kensington High Street in 1969, and finally, in the '70s, to a palatial 1930s department store further along the High Street. As Biba grew, it maintained its original blend of intimacy and grandeur; it reproduced the gleaming marble expanses of ballrooms in sepia musicals, yet was dotted with tiny inglenooks and private niches sprouting Edwardian potted palms.

Biba was a microcosm in which a "total look" was available via shoes, make-up, accessories, lingerie, and clothing of all descriptions for every occasion. Biba was famous for stocking newly minted pantyhose in a full color range, while Biba's boots were a sine qua non: "We used to queue up for them," recalls Marion Foale. "Oh, boy, they've got mauve ones this week!"

During Biba's earliest days, the Mod ensemble had been a uniform of what sociologists describe as "counter-conformity"—a common denominator of rebellion. "The fact that you had that dress said you were in," recalls Hulanicki. "You were breaking away from the old guard. It was a sign of prestige, even though you'd paid nothing for it." In the subsequent incarnations of the store in the later '60s, she saw a flowering of individuality that resonated with Biba's expanding size and wonderland ambience. "The more theatrical a place is, the more histrionic the dress and behavior becomes. One could just sit in that shop and watch how the customers handled the clothes: 'My goodness, what's she doing it with it now?!' I mean it was just incredible."

By 1969, Biba was "as much a tourist attraction . . . as the Tower of London," Britain's

Nova magazine claimed. Biba's spell was as intoxicating to its mistress as to the nearly 100,000 shoppers who, by 1969, passed through its doors in an average week. "I loved to go wafting through the store," recalls Hulanicki, who currently resides in Miami Beach and designs hotel and nightclub interiors, costumes rock videos, produces a wholesale line of children's wear, and is writing a novel to be published in Britain in 1990. "There's nothing more exciting than being in touch with the public," Hulanicki says. "It's like acting on the stage as opposed to film. I couldn't stand wholesale, because it's just between you and the buyer, and the buyers are always wrong, anyway. They want what sold last year, but we were working right on the moment, all the time."

Biba on a Saturday afternoon was likened to "the Swinging London branch of the Tower of Babel." Continental couturiers joined the stream of foreign visitors sampling the cacophony of London's renaissance. For some, these trips were productive reconnaissance missions; for others they were unsettling voyages into treacherous shoals. When Dior's Marc Bohan and Philip Guibourge returned from a London sortie in May 1966, they confessed that they were impressed by the crackling vigor of Swinging London, but unpersuaded nonetheless. Bohan said: "A couturier's job is dressing a woman, making her elegant. . . . Our client cannot wear those things and look beautiful." Nor could the fashion plates of Mod London have found much in the couture that would not have made them feel anachronistic and straitjacketed.

Eighteen-year-old Sally Hill Brookes attending the Ascot races in head-to-knee zig-zags, June 1966

Designer Zandra Rhodes in an Ossie Clark suit of polyvinyl chloride—one of the new synthetics introduced by Mary Quant and her colleagues—and a James Wedge medallion helmet; her companion here is Alex MacIntyre.

25

The weekend color supplements to London's daily newspapers were an important venue for the dissemination of the new fashions. David Bailey photographed Jean Shrimpton wearing Mary Quant for the cover of the start-up supplement to London's Sunday Times *in April 1962.*

(Right) Moderately priced "fun" furs, such as this Mongolian lamb coat, were the preferred pelt of London's young trendsetters, who reviled the status hides of the rich. Later in the decade, all fur would be shunned as ecological consciousness took hold.

(Far right) The "poor boy" sweater was championed by the ready-to-wear designers of London as well as Paris.

Susannah York mugs in a pluperfect Mod ensemble.

The new idols, actress Susannah York among them, were for the most part casual. York recalls attending the premiere of her first major film, *A Loss of Innocence*. "The movie had been made in France, and the invitation read: 'Come as you would to a gay summer evening in Southern France.' 'Well, I'm not going to wear shorts,' I thought, 'but I'll find a nice summer frock.' I bought some very pretty floral cotton, and asked my landlady to make a dress out of it. My husband and I went off happily on our motorscooter to Leicester Square, arriving forty-five minutes early, as we'd been asked to do. We were greeted by the movie pundits with absolute shock, horror, and dismay—apparently, I should have been in a long gown and arrived in a limousine. I stood in the foyer in floods of tears as they told me: 'You must go home and change! You are the *star* of this movie!' I stomped my foot and refused to go back. I can remember the absolute upset and humiliation of being told I didn't look like a movie star. I'd no idea what a movie star looked like."

Incorrigibly cheeky and irreverent, Mary Quant nonetheless became the grand old lady of contemporary London style during the mid '60s. "I am eternally grateful to her," designer Caroline Charles professed in 1964. "She opened up the way for a younger school of designers and made everything possible for us." In 1961, Quant had begun manufacturing her clothes for wholesale distribution. In 1963, she unveiled a second Bazaar, in London's posh Knightsbridge district. That year she also inaugurated her Ginger Group, a lower-priced line that spread her gospel to a wider audience than the unconventional but still economically empowered clientele who had frequented her original Bazaar. By the mid '60s, Quant was designing sewing patterns, rainwear, stockings, underwear, swimwear, nightgowns, furs, and cosmetics in addition to her seasonal collections for the London Bazaars, as well as for American and English wholesale accounts.

In the wake of the Beatles' invasion came an influx of Mod fashions into American markets. By the end of 1965, Paraphernalia was stocking the work of Quant and Foale and Tuffin; the boutique attached to New York's Cheetah discotheque featured imports from Biba. John Bates's clothes for "The Avengers," a stylish and slyly humorous spy-thriller television series, brought a graphically monochromatic Mod profile into the homes of its American viewers. Jean

(LEFT) Julie Christie with Harold Wilson; Wilson cultivated an aggressively contemporary image during his first term as Prime Minister, 1964 to 1970.

(BELOW) "What Julie Christie wears has more real impact on fashion than all the clothes of the ten Best-Dressed Women combined," Time noted in 1967.

Ian Gray, managing director of Carnaby Street's Gear boutique, and his wife, Ann, wear suits studded with "Dotties" in homage to the traditional garb of the Cockney "Pearly King and Queen."

Shrimpton, London's most celebrated model, was now "one of Britain's major assets and exports," the *New York Times* calculated.

Harold Wilson's Labour government as well as the Crown publicly acknowledged the benefits to the Empire—in export revenue and publicity—that Swinging clothes, like the music of the Beatles, provided. At Buckingham Palace in 1966, Quant was invested with the Order of the British Empire. "I was a bit horrified at first because I thought my friends would tease me," she later admitted, "but now I feel sort of respectable. We were sneered at for so long by the industry because they thought we were just a quick fad, and the O.B.E. seemed to prove we'd done something they hadn't believed possible."

In 1967, Jonathan Aitken wrote in *The Young Meteors* that "In the final analysis, it seems probable that the fashion revolution is the most significant influence on the mood and

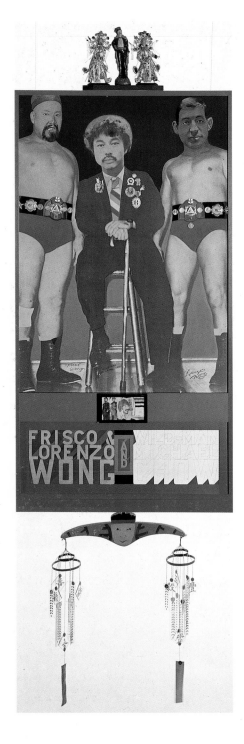

Peter Blake's portrait of restaurateur Michael Chow, commissioned for the interior of Mr. Chow's, the Knightsbridge restaurant that celebrated London's melting pot of internationalism in the '60s

mores of the younger generation in the last decade. . . . Britain's capital has been given a completely new image at home and abroad." The city reveled in its sartorial license. "At the moment," Georgina Howell declared in the *Observer* in January 1966, "it's the only place where anybody can wear anything they like and get away with it." London's rejuvenation was marketed by the media for international audiences. In the spring of 1966, *Time* saluted Swinging London in a cover story headlined, "You Can Walk Across It on the Green." The most dynamic catalysts of London's renaissance were themselves bewildered, however, by the hyperbole. "'What is this label? What is all this fuss?' we asked ourselves," Marian Foale recalls, "and then, oh boy, there were Americans everywhere asking for interviews."

The inevitable result of the *Time* article and a deluge of similar exposure was to calcify a phenomenon that had already, in truth, begun to turn a bit self-conscious. In October 1966, "Miniskirts or kinky gear" were requested for the London opening of the American film *Kaleidoscope*, starring Susannah York opposite Warren Beatty. Playing the owner of a swinging Chelsea boutique, York was clothed in Foale and Tuffin's finest. A prize of a hundred pounds was offered for the most outlandish outfit. *WWD* reported: "Even Leicester Square [pretty blasé] reeled under the impact of the flashing silver glitter and plastic . . . and the feather boas and the [wildly bottomed] trouser suits."

Carnaby Street had become overrun with tourists; the pedestrian arcade was now a global buzzword signifying an ersatz brand of "switched-on" garb. The British cognoscenti were rejecting Carnaby's rather crass aesthetic in no uncertain terms. "We are not in the least trendy or Mod," insisted Janet Lyle and Maggie Keswick on a trip to New York in 1966. Since their skirts climbed above their knees, Americans could be forgiven for thinking otherwise, but a glossary of fine distinctions was, as always, necessary for deciphering London's ever-changing social and sartorial milieu. At their South Kensington boutique, Annacat, Lyle and Keswick in 1965 began retailing billowing blouses with leg-of-mutton sleeves and stock ties. Yet another alternative was proposed by Jean Muir, who became the darling of sophisticated American merchandisers for her tailored, upscale wardrobe.

Leading an about-face from hard-edged Mod toward a softer, more impressionistic mode was a cadre of romantics reclaiming the legacy of earlier bohemian and blue-blooded champions of dress reform. The intransigent dreamers of the '60s recalled the nineteenth-century muses of the Pre-Raphaelites, as well as the wild cards of the 1920s, most prominent among them poetess Nancy Cunard. Heiress to the shipping fortune, Cunard had flaunted a wardrobe designed by Sonia Delauney, armfuls of African ivory bracelets, and (in addition) a black lover—all to the horror of her mother, Emerald, a famed hostess. The generation of the mid

Chrissie Shrimpton, seen here in 1967, was the sister of supermodel Jean Shrimpton and the steady flame of Mick Jagger.

(RIGHT) Top model Celia Hammond's fair hair and pale lips epitomized the London look of the mid '60s.

'60s took up the gauntlet thrown down by such progenitors. High on the agenda of this new breed was promoting the beauty and authenticity of vintage and ethnic clothing. "Anything fitted or with buttons was suspect," writer Joan Juliet Buck recalls. "We had this tremendous longing for knotty authenticity—the lure of the East. We actually believed that we were those student beggar princesses or advance scouts for the Indian army." "English youth is deserting Carnaby Street in favor of the Portobello Road," *Life* noted in December 1966. Though destined to become a fashion metaphor, this London street of antique stalls was then "no fashion center but a flea market of some twenty years standing," *Life* informed its American readers.

No individual seemed more truly a successor to the aristocratic iconoclasts of yore than the Honorable Jane Ormsby-Gore. "I'm very anarchistic, I would say," recalls this prime mover of the revolt of British upper-class youth during the '60s. Ormsby-Gore is the scioness of a distinguished Celtic dynasty. Her late father, Lord David Harlech, was successively British delegate to the United Nations and ambassador to the U.S. during Kennedy's presidency. Ormsby-Gore today works for London interior decorator David Milinaric and runs her own Fieldhouse home furnishings shop. Regally tall, with large dark eyes and a stunning aquiline face,

Twiggy in a double-breasted trouser suit from Bagatel, 1968

she frequently created a sensation, even in Swinging London. "I'll never forget the first time she came into Biba," recalls Barbara Hulanicki. "Jane had on a pair of jeans cropped at the ankle, onto which she had sewn red bobble lampshade fringe. The whole store started whispering: 'Come and see this girl!'" In 1966, Ormsby-Gore married Michael Rainey, proprietor of the Hung on You boutique of King's Road. Her wedding costume was an antique lace chemise, accessorized with fresh flowers strewn through her raven-black hair. Ormsby-Gore's publicly expressed preference for cast-off clothes raised many eyebrows, including those belonging to the staff of British *Vogue*, where she came to edit the "Shop Hound" pages during the mid

Joan Juliet Buck in a mélange of thrift-store clothes

'60s. But Ormsby-Gore, like her sisters Victoria and Alice and brother Julian, was an invincible propagandist. Described by the *Daily Sketch* as "one of the most startling and exotically geared families around London," the Ormsby-Gores persuaded by virtue of their unconventional beauty, exotic flair, and noble bloodlines.

"It didn't seem to be that extraordinary to look like one did," she recalls, "because—suddenly—everything was being broken down. I would say the great thing about the '60s was

Jane Rainey watching an Ossie Clark fashion show in 1967, accompanied by her infant son Saffron

the huge erosion of social strata," she estimates. "I always longed not to be contained within my class." Ormsby-Gore was raised on the family estate in Wales:

My father was the local MP for years, so there was always this huge cross-section at our house. We were given a terrific scope of freedom—comparative to those around us. What happened after the war, you see, was that the traditions of Victorian England were very much brought back to stabilize everybody, especially in the upper classes. It was very rigid. It seems as though we were very extraordinary and extravagant, but really, it was that everybody else was so deeply boring and conventional.

I remember one weekend when I was fifteen or sixteen we had Princess Margaret coming to stay, and a lot of grand servants 'specially come for the weekend. One night all the furniture was pushed back in the drawing room and everybody started rocking and rolling. My eyes popped out of my head—"My God, this is nice!" It all was just beginning.

When her father was dispatched to Washington, she was reluctant to forfeit the latitude of her life in a reawakening Britain. "I was longing not to go, because America then was still so straight and boring." Much to her chagrin, "in America I had to wear long white gloves and go to balls, and, oh, I couldn't stand it!" Upon her expeditious return to England, interior decorator Christopher Gibbs wrote in British *Vogue*:

She does, it is true, buy a few clothes from boutiques like Biba, Dandy and Deliss, but under her expert eye, they suffer a sea change. She hates a well-chosen, carefully accessorized outfit, preferring to decorate what she wears with dozens of chains, rings, vast shimmering cufflinks, and festoons of strange rare flowers.

Psychedelia descended into London in 1966–67: the lush tactility, verdant palette, and eclectic assembly fermented by San Francisco took the British capital by storm. In August 1967, Felicity Green reported in the *Daily Mirror* that "The kooky kids of '66 have been replaced by the flower girls of '67. Swinging London is awash with Hippie fashions." 1967 was the annus mirabilis of standing "against status and money and the recognizeable object," recalls Joan Juliet Buck, one of the British daughters of affluence who rebelled against her birthright. "The Hermès bags my mother gave me I would pass along very fast."

During the boom years of the mid '60s, King's Road swiftly shed the sleepy amicability that had prevailed when Mary Quant threw open her doors a decade earlier. The invasion of Mary Quant and Kiki Byrne released a floodtide—a swath of boutiques unfurling for block after

London's Take 6 boutique installed
artist Vere Smith to paint clothes purchased at the
shop to customers' specifications.

London hippie at a Hyde Park happening in July 1967

an exotic black tulle, imprinted with silver tracery—"the sort of thing that Theda Bara wore in *Cleopatra*, and a great favorite of Sarah Bernhardt." Adjacent to the Emmerton-Lambert boutique was a cafe, with a sheltered terrace overlooking King's Road. "One could sit there all day long and not be harrassed," he recalls. It was thus the perfect hideaway for Hendrix or Jagger or the anonymous acid-tripper.

Responding to the renewed interest, wondrous caches of old clothes were suddenly surfacing all over London and its environs. Large department stores conducted divestment auctions. Out of cold storage appeared the long-forgotten trunks of deceased marchionesses and duchesses, or the vintage furs of a legendary screen goddess. Amateur playhouses in the provinces marketed trunks of eighteenth-century clothes donated by local demesnes. Slumbering warehouses were perused—in a storehouse outside Paris, a long-lost stockpile of Diaghilev's costumes was unearthed and auctioned at Sotheby's.

A frequent visitor to Lambert's boutique was a Chelsea resident whose grandmother had boarded Oscar Wilde's children the night he was arrested at his home across the street from her. The matriarch had also been a mistress of Edward VII. "Granny's things are all still there in the attic," her descendent told Lambert, who duly reported to the family home in nearby Tite Street. "The trunks were opened, and you can imagine what her clothes were like."

"England being such a convervative country, it had never experienced a fiesta," declares Lambert. "There'd always been pageantry, yes, but not a carnival atmosphere. But then the summer of 1967 was one long party, and all the dress-up boxes in the attic all came out. People were going to the supermarket in the morning in Granny's Poirets and Chanels. The King's Road was a fantasy promenade every day, a party. The sky was the limit."

PARIS

London's rise was paralleled by the fall of Paris as the world's fashion capital. During the '60s the French luxury made-to-order industry suffered its most trying identity crisis of the century. Left-wing political movements challenged the elitism the couture symbolized. Insurgent elements in ready-to-wear stole the lead in design innovation. Young designers who had been nurtured by the couture system began to call for its abolition.

There was a fundamental incompatibility between the new woman emerging in the '60s and the couture's traditional clientele. "It may be that this time feminine emancipation is irreversible," costume historian James Laver predicted in 1964. "There are signs of this—woman being the breadwinner, the woman earning more than the man. . . . We are now on the eve of something very extraordinary in the way of social set up." Yet the raison d'etre of the couture was still the fastidious creature of old, a clotheshorse with boundless means. Given the limited economic opportunities available to women during the '50s and much of the '60s, the couture's typical clientele was a famous entertainer, a member of European royalty or the wife of a present-day Croesus. She was an *élégante* with the time and patience to endure repeated, painstaking custom fittings, a woman whose fascination with her own appearance was all-consuming, whose energy was channeled into the physical perfection of self and home. The traditional couture remained, for the most part, immune to the new paths women were exploring during the '60s. "To make a definite statement—to say that one thing is the look—is démodé," Gerard Pipart, maestro of the Nina Ricci couture house said in 1967. "But I can see very definitely in Europe that the business about the emancipated woman, the free woman is no more." Ensconced in its ivory tower, the old couture could not very well be anything but blind to women's new directions; they precluded the old loyalties and demanded a re-ordering of priorities.

Yet during the '60s another class of French couturiers emerged, denouncing the wonted practices as oppressive and outmoded. They recognized the end of the pampered woman. The Young Turks called for the overhaul of their own industry. "Look at how we have failed," André Courrèges berated in 1963. "Look at a man's suit, how much more logical, realistic and contemporary than women's clothes." In 1969, Emanuel Ungaro discussed his ideal customer. She was not a grand dame idling in a jet or yacht; she was "the woman who now exists in Paris . . . that you see on the streets here. . . . She has a great desire to seize and grasp a life. She knows within her that she must survive and earn a living and she wants to succeed."

During the '50s, the oligarchy of Paris couture had been enveloped in the mystique of an insulated, Olympian citadel deploying lightning bolt fiats. The couture held sway over Western dress during the '50s, influencing not only what private customers wore but the dress of mul-

A rakish take on Dietrich from Marc Bohan's spring 1966 couture collection for the House of Dior

Vicomtesse Jacqueline de Ribes epitomized the haute couture *patroness of the '50s and early '60s.*

titudes many tiers further down the economic scale. British and U.S. manufacturers set their watches by couture, traveling to Paris twice a year to purchase at specially inflated prices garments they would then adapt for a mass audience.

The tenor of '50s couture was established in 1947 with Christian Dior's "New Look," a cataclysm that made the boxy silhouette of the '40s obsolete overnight. In reaction to half a decade of wartime restrictions, Dior employed intricate seaming and darting, layer upon layer of interfacing, to construct an exaggerated hourglass configuration—a throwback almost to the turn of the century. "Each of his dresses, lined throughout, was like a piece of architecture that rested upon its foundations," writes Françoise Giroud in *Christian Dior*. During the '50s, Dior became the world's most famous couturier, ruling a vast empire that included a ready-to-wear satellite in New York. His major rival was the Spaniard Cristóbal Balenciaga. The two masters worked on parallel poles with reverse charges: both were shape oriented, but while Dior each season conjured a novel sculpted, constructed silhouette, Balenciaga seasonally evolved a blousy, smocky, partially fitted daytime shape. Balenciaga's evening clothes wafted around the body, bells and butterfly wings carved from heavy failles and satins.

While the caprices of the private client were legendary, most women came to the couture deferring to the taste of a recognized arbiter; despite the flexibility offered by custom-made designs, couture was not for self-expression. Marella Agnelli, wife of the Fiat automobile titan, recalled in 1977 how, after her marriage, she "had to be elegant. . . . Mr. Balenciaga was my defense. One presented an image invented by someone else, which was marvelous."

As much as design, the couture purveyed mystique, the aura of centuries of refinement and exclusivity. True to his heritage, Balenciaga demanded from the press and customers an ecclestiastical reverence. Dior's festive shower of luxury was opposed to Balenciaga's transformation of fashion design into the apprehension of divine epiphany. From the moment the visitor stepped into the elevator to the master's salon, she was made aware of the privilege of her admittance to hallowed ground. "I can still recall that terrible lift," remembers Barbara Hulanicki, who visited Balenciaga's salon frequently while working during the '50s as an illustrator for the London print media. "It was lined in glossy plum leather with brass studs. You could just get two or three people in at a squash. It was like going into a padded cell."

Guarding the portals of the couture were press attachés, "dragons who made life as difficult as possible," Felicity Green, formerly fashion editor for London's *Daily Mail*, recalls. Importuning these sentinels as to who would see, sketch, or photograph a collection, and at what time, were futile:

"You can't come till Wednesday next week," Green was told.

"But I have to come today because I work on a daily paper."

"Je ne parle pas anglais."

Even during times of genuine upheaval, fashion progresses along evolutionary lines as much as cataclysmic trajectories. Although Balenciaga was out of step with the '60s, he had prefigured the loose, unconfining chemise—cornerstone of the decade's fashion—when he began relaxing the waist in 1951. In 1954, Gabrielle Chanel returned to couture following a fifteen-year respite. With their relative lack of construction, Chanel's cardigan suits seemed

Saint Laurent putting the finishing touches on a design
in his fall 1962 couture collection.

anachronistic, yet as the '50s progressed, they became the core of many women's wardrobes, and Chanel's pastel tweed ensembles were the acme of sprightly ease.

The return of the unfitted shape in the late '50s can be seen not only as the inevitable swing of the fashion pendulum, but as a particularly significant augury. For the chemise had long been invested with liberal connotations. In the wake of the industrial revolution, field laborers discarded the smock, which was then adopted by the avant-garde of the 1880s and 1890s, the dress-reforming ideologues of the Arts and Crafts movement, who used it to protest the meretricious opulence of the machine age. In the 1920s the waistless dress was the perfect symbol of the flapper's frenetic transgression of restriction and taboo.

The softer, less forbidding late '50s looks of such houses as Ricci, Lanvin, and the newly opened Cardin revealed a growing awareness of the coming of age of the postwar baby boom generation. In 1957, Dior's Young Collection debuted in America, where the teenage market was already booming. In Paris, several couture houses had opened ready-to-wear boutiques on their premises. Among them was Hubert de Givenchy; his direction of Audrey Hepburn's wardrobe garnered the couturier exposure among the sophisticated youth who idolized her.

The rate at which the couture was moving seemed glacial, however, to a new sisterhood of female designers who began early in the '60s to exploit the opportunities offered by France's burgeoning clothing manufacturing industry. A 1966 survey suggested that in the early '50s, as much as 85 percent of French women's clothing had been made by hand; fifteen years later more than two-thirds was factory produced. The new designers would be known as the "yé-yé" school, after the idiomatic pronunciation by French teenagers of the Beatles' "Yeah, yeah, yeah."

"Haute couture is dead," twenty-six-year-old Emmanuelle Khanh announced in 1964. "I want to design for the street . . . a socialist kind of fashion for the grand mass." The lodestar of French ready-to-wear, Khanh had become involved with fashion eight years earlier. A Parisian orphan, she wanted to model, consulted the phonebook under the listing *couture*, and called the first name on the list—Balenciaga. While modeling for Givenchy and Balenciaga, Khanh designed and made her own fashions, which elicited the interest of *Elle* journalists. They asked to photograph her clothes for the magazine and interested a manufacturer in producing them. Khanh stopped modeling in 1961 and turned her full attention to designing. In 1962, the fabric manufacturer Lalonde sponsored a collection of the designs of Khanh and Christiane Bailly, also an ex-Balenciaga model. The "Emmachristie" collection "was the blueprint for the yé-yé revolution," Marilyn Bender records in 1967's *The Beautiful People*. By 1964, Khanh was doing collections for four French coat and suit manufacturers, three in

Emmanuelle Khanh wearing her own designs on a visit to New York in 1964

England and one in West Germany. Her clothes were brought to the U.S. by Macy's Shanna Simon and J. C. Penney's Paul Young, who hired her to design special collections for their stores.

Intrepid buyers and reporters negotiated five flights of winding, groaning stairs to visit the new meteor in her two-room apartment on the Rue St. Honoré. Hinged hardwood pieces of the floor opened to reveal sunken mattresses. A television set hung in a cubbyhole between two rooms, revolving slowly on a rope. It was purely decorative, Khanh explained—never turned on: it reflected the fascination for technology she shared with her husband, Nguyen, a Vietnamese engineer.

"They make Rolls Royces," Khanh said, elucidating her dissatisfaction with couture, "very chic you know, but stable, unmoving. . . . Haute couture clothes are beautiful but you see the beauty of the clothes, not the beauty of the body," she complained. Peering through round lenses in the tortoiseshell frames she designed, Khanh had the diffident air of a university undergraduate, but nonetheless issued fighting words with the fervor of a Joan of Arc. On her first trip to New York in 1964, she recalled her modeling days: "Balenciaga treated us like chairs and I think the fact that he couldn't care less about us—women—reflects on the way he creates dresses."

Though opposed to the aristocratic bulwark behind which Chanel functioned, Khanh saw herself as that designer's acolyte in creating clothes that freed and highlighted the body. Khanh described her method: "Cut is everything. I cut the sleeves to suggest the curve of the arm, the skirt to suggest the hips. Clothes must move when a woman moves."

"I want to feminize fashion to the maximum," said Khanh. She cut elliptical sleeves and used asymmetrical closings to counterpoint the seams she wound sinuously around her garments. Her idiosyncratic details became famous: droopy, "dog's ear" lapels, truncated sleeves, and turned-back cuffs. Khanh's penchant for Harris tweeds and Shetland wools reflected an Anglophile orientation long present in the daytime dress of middle-class French-women of all ages. Helmets and goggles were among the accoutrements she used to distill the sensual, independent woman crystallized in the contemporaneous New Wave cinema.

"Things have never been the same since Courrèges had his explosion," Yves Saint Laurent confessed in 1966, alluding to the cataclysm that catapulted the couture into the '60s. After ten years as head tailor at Balenciaga, André Courrèges had struck out on his own in 1961. He set up shop in a humble atelier two flights above a courtyard on the Avenue Kléber. For several years Courrèges produced collections reflecting in varying degrees Balenciaga's influence. Then, in January 1964, Courrèges made his breakthrough, irrevocably parting with colleagues engrossed in the lengthening shadow of the couture's days of autocratic dominance. The spring 1964 collections were steeped in homages to "the glorious days" of the 1930s, when "Paris was elegant, romantic and outwardly restrained . . . when clothes were . . . neat and always feminine." Amid the flood of suits inspired by the '30s *tailleurs* of Molyneux and Chanel, Courrèges unveiled a collection unprecedently spare and unadorned. He propounded graphically etched pinafore dresses and suits with hemlines well above the knee. The bedrock of his collection, however, were pants worn for day and evening, city and country. They were slit at the inseam to present an exaggerated elongation, or cut perpendicular to the fabric's grain to suggest the fuselage of a rocket ship. Courrèges's collection was singularly devoid of the furbelows that connoted "female" in most of the couture. The Courrèges ideal was "a modern girl who has journeyed through ancient Sparta," Violette Le Duc wrote in French *Vogue*. His heroine was lean, well-muscled, and bra-less. Courrèges's militancy sparked a fervid debate over pants. "Conservative buyers are terrified to buy Courrèges before they see

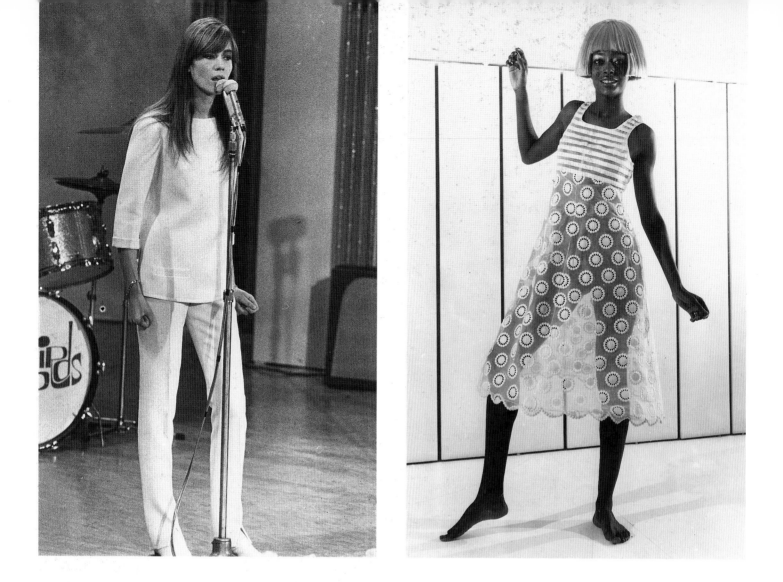

what B [Balenciaga] and G [Givenchy] are going to do," *WWD* noted that February. Norman Norell, dean of Seventh Avenue designers, had been showing casual trouser and culotte suits for some time. Nonetheless, he affirmed his belief that women in pants should not venture beyond the private sphere. "It would scare me to hell . . . just think, a man comes from his office—his wife jumps into her pants to go out to dinner and so does he." Courrèges's endorsement went a long way toward advancing the acceptance of pants for all occasions, which had become widespread by the end of the '60s. In August 1964, London's Tuffin and Foale reported on their trouser suits: "We had a big battle with buyers over them, 'till Paris did them. Now they're screaming for them."

Accompanied by the throbbing tatoo of African tom-toms, Courrèges orchestrated an overwhelming presentation in January 1965 that was an even bolder expression of his aesthetic. Chevron stitching at the hips of dresses and pants heightened an eroticism that was as unforgettable to spectators as the blinding glare of his salon. Its niveous blaze was the departure point for a renunciation of all the appurtenances of traditional couture. The designer was not

(LEFT) Françoise Hardy in a Courrèges couture wool pantsuit, 1966

(RIGHT) In his spring 1969 couture collection, Courrèges highlighted a white organdy evening dress with blue embroidered motifs, worn with a Dynel wig.

Evening clothes from Emmanuelle Khanh's fall 1965 collection for manufacturer I.D. A top of fluorescent plastic squares appliquéd to crêpe, over flared crêpe trousers by Dorothée Bis (left). Khanh's halter-neck dress with matching gilet (right).

49

reluctant to use freaky, comical exaggeration to put his points across. In contrast to ladylike pillboxes, he showed futuristic platter hats, bonnets, or helmets. He demonstrated his disdain for the spindly stiletto heel by advocating his famous white glacé boots and then flat Mary-Jane slippers. "It is not logical . . . to work all day on three-inch heels," Courrèges said. "Men should try it and they'll soon find out. . . . Heels are as absurd as the bound feet of ancient orientals."

Courrèges's mode of presentation was diametrically opposed to the couture status quo. Balenciaga's models, the *New York Times*'s Gloria Emerson observed in 1968, "never give a grin, a toss of the head, an extra pivot or an extra pause. They march in and out of the salons like little soldiers with an invisible master sergeant counting cadence." By contrast, Courrèges's models leapt and frugged in a perpetual motion of violent exertion. Courrèges was a consummate showman and enjoyed pulling out all the stops. In January 1968, he employed Guadaloupan dancer Gérald Félix to bolt out of one of the white leather cubes on which the press corps was seated awaiting the start of the show. In a flash, Félix had peeled down to white jersey boxer shorts and dissapeared behind white screens ressembling radar antennaa through which his shadow swayed alluringly to a drum obliggato during the course of the proceedings.

Unfortunately, Courrèges was not immune to the occupational paranoia of the couture. His designs were a clear, easily disseminated prototype, and the couturier chafed at the armies of fascsimile Courrèges marching around the world (without acknowledging his own debt to London ready-to-wear). Once again he astounded the fashion world when he insisted he would no longer stage shows for the press or retail buyers but would now sell only to private clients. Courrèges's sabbatical would, he explained, allow him to raise the funding needed to begin his own ready-to-wear operation. "Working women have always interested me the most," Courrèges had said in the spring of 1965. "They belong to the present, the future." He envisioned his original designs becoming available to a wider cross-section than the couture attracted. "I perfectly well realize how utterly immoral my high prices are." For two years he searched for backers while making clothes for private clients. Cheered on by sympathizers in the fashion avant-garde, Courrèges returned to press showings in January 1967 with a dual collection of couture and ready-to-wear. "Courrèges is so strong that he could go away for 50 years, come back and still be with it," Betsey Johnson exclaimed. But in the two years since his last showing, fashion had catapulted past his own early trajectory. Courrèges said his dresses were designed for the wearer's maximum ease: "the functional must be the soul of a dress, its composition, its interior rhythm. . . . Aesthetics is the envelope." But Courrèges

Courrèges wool dress from his ready-to-wear collection in 1967

Two views of Yves Saint Laurent's Mondrian-inspired group of wool jersey dresses from his fall 1965 couture collection

relied upon the hard, tailored wools he had worked with at Balenciaga. Courrèges had received an engineering degree before turning to fashion, and his clothes authored a new architecture, predicated on the flaring triangle of his skirts and his attenuated tubular pants. Akin to the spaceship in its white and silver accents, emphatically outlined by welt seaming, Courrèges's once radical silhouette was now itself anachronistic. He did not return with a drastically different look, but one that, like Balenciaga's, evolved naturally.

Some were disappointed at the fine tuning he had introduced. *WWD* mentioned "the irony between frilliness of new details and simplicity of line and basic fabrics. . . . Often he softened unwillingly, it seemed, and in haste to get it over with." Yet Courrèges was never static; as the '60s ended, he continued to pioneer, employing the body stocking or jumpsuit as the heart of supremely flexible modular wardrobes.

The same designer who in 1983 would call for a return to the "immense prestige and the immense luxury of the 1950s" had been ardently sketching the insurgent students at the Paris barricades in 1968. Yves Saint Laurent's impressionability has been his greatest gift and his most egregious failing. He is a sensitive seismograph, but his statements are often diffused by his frequent vacillations. During the '60s Saint Laurent ratified renegade idioms; he was, as Deborah Silverman writes in *Selling Culture*, "a great adapter . . . one of the first designers to respond to countercultural movements and to incorporate them into his fashions." He created two landmark couture collections that bracketed the decade's cultural and political foment. In July 1960, while steering the house of Dior after the death of its founder, his beat collection virtually launched the '60s in Paris by its appropriation of Left Bank raiment. Eight years later, he responded to the May student uprisings with a severely tailored pants collection that reflected the egalitarian garb of the striking students. During most of the decade, however, Saint Laurent's work was a compromise between the revolutionary aesthetics of vanguard design and the anachronistic creations of the old guard in which he been reared. At eighteen Saint Laurent had became Dior's assistant. Though he was the same age as the jackanapes of ready to wear, Saint Laurent had already been molded by a different school, one in which the real configuration of the female body was concealed. "A woman had only to step into a Dior evening gown; the interior scaffolding did the rest," Barbara Schreier writes in *Mystique and Identity: Women's Fashions of the 1950s*.

During the '60s, Saint Laurent seemed torn between his allegiance to the tenets of classical couture and his fascination with the daring and freedom introduced by the new generation of designers. On the eve of his spring 1966 showing, St. Laurent related: "This season I am bursting with the desire to go much further and revolutionize everything. Then I think: it would be perfect for the Saint Germain des Prés boutique, at say, $100 . . . but at couture prices will they accept it?"

Throughout the decade, Saint Laurent seemed cognizant of the revolution but not quite sure how to position himself in the continously shifting terrain: "There has been an immense upheaval in the last three years," he said in 1966. "Most women have not been able to keep up. They still think the wealthy look will solve everything. . . . Niki de Saint-Phalle in a 10-franc dress bought at Les Puces [the Parisian flea market] has more real elegance than many women dressed in the haute couture."

His populist leanings were belied by the elite traditions to which his house held fast. As of August 1967, his prices were the steepest in Paris (along with Balenciaga's). "Saint Laurent is young, imaginative, and creative," opined Rudi Gernreich in 1966. "But why should his Pop clothes cost so much?"

Saint Laurent's attempts at relevance throughout the '60s made him a lightning rod for criticism of the paucity of originality in the couture. "Everyone knows Saint Laurent has been ripping off the kids' street gear for years and even those knock-off waves of his roll in about six months to a year too late," Blair Sabol lambasted in a 1970 *Village Voice* article. To American retailers, however, most of his collections during the '60s came as manna from heaven; he replaced Balenciaga as their favorite. "Saint Laurent has a special mystique for this country," Eugenia Sheppard noted in 1968. His clothes were just hip enough: the sportswear look he promoted was easily permeable by the lexicon of youthful vernacular, but also kept a Chanel-like neatness. "My trick is to bring the couture up to date but still not make it look like boutique," he explained after showing his spring 1966 collection, in which he incorporated see-through cocktail dresses as well as fashions inspired by the Army-Navy stores he had inspected on his visit to New York the previous fall.

In 1965, J. Mack Robinson, an American insurance executive, sold his majority interest in the House of Saint Laurent to the giant cosmetics firm Lanvin–Charles of the Ritz. The harness imposed by Saint Laurent's new corporate allegiance determined that he weight his collections with dresses that were, he explained in 1968, targeted for the tastes of individual store buyers. "Saint Laurent dreams of being a hippie," G. Y. Dryansky reported in *WWD* in January 1968, "and sticks to being Saint Laurent in large part because of what comes across as an honest sense of responsibility—to the people around him, to the people backing him."

Saint Laurent was the couturier of choice for many of the rising French film and music stars, who were very young and for the most part uninterested in the old couture. In the '30s,

Chanel was recruited by Hollywood to round off the sartorial edges of its sirens; she could not, however, exert a similar influence over the most iconic star of the early '60s. "Dress at my house and I will make you into an elegant woman," Chanel reportedly promised Brigitte Bardot. "Elegance? I couldn't care less. It's old fashioned," Bardot replied, who bought most of her clothes off the peg. "Couture is for grannies," Bardot protested.

After selecting several Saint Laurent couture models in October 1966, singer Françoise Hardy was observed to change back into a navy sailor's sweater and a miniskirt she had purchased for $4 at the Paris boutique Elle. Hardy typified the affluent and restless new generation that freely shunted between the worlds of privelege and pluralism. Her dégagé, melancholy mien enchanted French teenagers as much as her bittersweet ballads. In 1967, Cecil Beaton wrote that it was Hardy "whom I would nominate as exemplifying the look of today.

From Ungaro's fall 1969 couture collection: a silver lamé jumpsuit covered with a black silk organza skirt decorated with metallic plastic bands in black circles, worn with a silver necklace

Roger Vivier boots shown with Ungaro's fall 1966 couture collection.

With her leather belt pulled into its last notch, soft sweet sweater and schoolboy's hat, her strands of drowned hair, her puma features, and long patterned stockings, she belongs to a young group that makes all earlier fashions seems fussy and frowsty [sic]."

The simply but perfectly turned face and style of Catherine Deneuve made her Saint Laurent's favorite bellwether. "It's she who makes the best liaison between 'le chic' . . . and the new manner of dressing," he said in 1967. "She is still very soignée." The actress explained

Floral panne velvet gown from Saint Laurent's fall 1969 couture collection

her patronage by describing Saint Laurent as "so young and fresh. . . . It's not couture as most people think of couture. . . . He's a camp. . . . His collection is not just so chic and chic and chic."

"The liberation must progress," Emanuel Ungaro insisted shortly before his spring 1966 couture collection opened. Speaking to *WWD*'s Thelma Sweetinburgh with a demeanor "as earnest as a terrorist," Ungaro extolled clothes that were similarly blunt. Like Courrèges, Ungaro had undergone a lengthy apprenticeship at Balenciaga. After six years with the Spanish couturier, he joined Courrèges's organization in 1964 before opening his own house a year later with a collection of twenty daywear models. "I won't be showing any evening dresses. This place isn't big enough for evening dresses, but even if I had three million francs I wouldn't do them. They are not my style." Several seasons later, he relented, with a dress studded with white styrofoam ping pong balls, a confection, the designer explained, "meant to destroy the idea of evening clothes."

Ungaro's clothes were for the new breed of women "who have become so strong and so independent. . . . I want girls to look healthy," he said, "sun-burnt . . . with sturdy legs to stand on. . . . I want them to look as though they had a good appetite."

His skirts were the shortest in the Paris couture. Like Courrèges, Ungaro championed the short length as the only one commensurate with vigorous activity. "Midi-skirts and boots are false romanticism," he complained in 1967. "It is not by wearing a skirt to the ankles that a girl becomes more romantic. It is only a disguise and there is a great deal of conformism in wearing such a disguise."

Unlike Courrèges, Ungaro preferred bold colors—pink and orange with turquoise, blue and green chased in red. The stunning fabrics Sonia Knapp designed exclusively for him were a trump card. Knapp's association with Ungaro began in 1962, when she was an art student in Zurich. Her textile designs became more and more painterly and less geometric as the sixties progressed, encompassing biomorphic abstractions that were compared to enlargement photographs of the moving Paris sky or wind-blown sea grass. Knapp deployed myriad shades of the same color to suggest the feathery drizzle of a blurred brushstroke. Fabrics that looked as though they had been appliquéd with abstract shapes of contrasting material were actually cut out of one piece of cloth. Rothko-like striations undulated in pinks and purples and browns and yellows. A pipeline to contemporary art was always present at Ungaro's salon, never more so than when he asked three top modern sculptors to design jewelry for his July 1968 couture

(ABOVE) A paper dress by Paco Rabanne causes consternation in a Left Bank boutique, 1967.

(RIGHT) Paco Rabanne with the evening dresses made from pink, green, and silver plastic discs, worn with matching earrings, that catapulted him to notoriety early in 1966.

showing. Fontana created bracelets, Giso Pomodoro made pendants and necklaces, and Oscar Guston designed free-form aluminum bras.

Ungaro used Oriental shadow plays to embroider upon the antic, athletic, and erotic mode of Courrèges's presentations. In January 1968, he darkened his salon to a single pinpoint of light. Posing briefly in the shaft of illumination, his models retreated to the rear of Ungaro's stage, turned their backs on the audience, and announced their numbers in sonorous tones. Six months later, Ungaro's show was again presented in projection-room blackness, with a transparent backdrop, like a Japanese *shoji* screen, lit from behind. A side wall of rotating cylinders, stainless steel on one side and mirrored on the reverse, abutted a black velvet stage with a pole in the center. Models sprung onto the stage, grasped the pole, and circled around it to show the clothes at all angles. In June 1969, he employed an electronic "télémégascope" to project onto a five-foot screen on the wall above the stage close-ups of the fanciful overlaid seaming on flaring coats and dresses that was his trademark.

"He hates all the chi-chi and the snobbishness that he thinks represents Paris to most people," Eugenia Sheppard reported in 1969. "The couture must have a new dimension," Ungaro said. "Some of the superficiality must go."

By the mid '60s, young Parisians were reaping the fruit of boutiques offering the cachet of topical fashion by ready-to-wear's new leaders. Dowagers and socialites flocked as well to these honeycomb storefronts around the Left Bank, of which Dorothée Bis, poised on the outskirts of Paris's bohemian quarter, was the heirloom seed. The boutique's proprietors, Jacqueline and Elie Jacobson, were among the first retailers to promote the endeavors of Khanh and her colleagues; in addition, Jacqueline Jacobson's own timely designs were featured amid a welter of aluminum-pipe racks and an aluminum ceiling. By 1966, Dorothée Bis had expanded into six franchised boutiques across Europe, and the couture was training an eagle eye on the successes across the Seine. Saint Laurent's youth and his appeal to the young made him the perfect candidate to inaugurate a ready-to-wear division that would be sold in his own franchised chain of boutiques. On the edge of the student quarter, Saint Laurent's pilot Rive Gauche boutique was unveiled in September 1966. Commenting on the advent of couturier's boutiques, Christiane Bailly said they made her "half proud because it proves we are right, and half displeased because couturiers have it too easy." Bailly complained that off-the-peg models were shown in the fashion glossies after the haute couture, so that "what we do sometimes looks like a copy of couture when we actually did it first." Bailly's nailhead dresses had proceeded the couture by six months.

Ready-to-wear star Michèle Rosier was the daughter of *Elle* publisher Hélène Lazareff; after a stint as a fashion journalist, she turned to design while retaining her reporter's eye. "Everything that happens in the streets and the love I have of it influences me," Rosier avowed in 1966. Her skiwear perpetuated the innovations in action wear triggered by Emilio Pucci's designs in the '50s; she was nicknamed "The Vinyl Girl" for her particular prediliction for the material. "Everything beautiful has the right to exist, the eccentric as well as the rational, provided it's cheap," she avowed.

A cult heroine of French prêt-à-porter was Sonia Rykiel. Starting out by designing her own maternity dresses, Rykiel began in 1964 to contribute designs to her husband's boutique, Laura, located in one of Paris's peripheral gateways, the Porte d'Orléans. Rykiel finessed the body-hugging, high-armhole knitted shape, which was ubiquitous among Paris boutiques, into a silhouette that struck a responsive chord in women around the world. "We used to traipse up there like it was a pilgrimage," Barbara Hulanicki recalls. When Audrey Hepburn paid her first visit to Laura in 1966, *WWD* reported that Hepburn had been "re-Audreyed . . . away from the heavy seaming, away from the stiffness" bestowed by her longtime exclusive patron-

Sonia Rykiel jersey dresses: from 1964 (above) and 1966 (opposite).

61

Evening hardware from Paco Rabanne

age of Givenchy. By 1970, "Sonia Rykiel" boutiques proliferated throughout the U.S. and Europe.

The rise of Paco Rabanne in 1966 followed an archetypal '60s scenario: in a lumpen setting an obscure designer detonated a fashion bombshell. In February 1966, in his fifth floor walk-up apartment, he unveiled a collection of dresses, vests, after-swim wear, and enormous bib necklaces all made of phosphorescent Rhodoid plastic discs strung with fine wire. "I defy anyone to design a hat, coat or dress that hasn't been done before. . . . The only new frontier left in fashion is the finding of new materials," Rabanne declared. Rabanne's explorations with plastic were the most sensational and media-intensive fashion event of that year.

Paco Rabanne was the son of Balenciaga's first seamstress in San Sebastian, Spain. He set out to be an architect, studying at the Atelier Pérette while working for Rojet Jean-Pierre, a jeweler for the haute couture. Givenchy featured Rabanne's aluminum jacket with bead pearls and amber pearls in 1960. "I showed Givenchy my plastic jewelry—it was a bit more crude then," Rabanne explained in 1966. "He was very kind and explained why it wouldn't do for the haute couture." He found a more receptive audience in the ready-to-wear triumvi-

Silver-chain halter dress by Paco Rabanne, 1967

63

Cardin lace and vinyl dress from his spring 1968
couture collection

Mannerist-influenced silk gazar dress from the House
of Patou, fall 1968

rate of Khanh, Bailly, and Rosier, each of whom began in 1962 showing his jewelry and accessories with their collections. In July 1966, Rabanne showed twelve new models of leather, aluminum, ostrich feathers, and Rhodoid plastic at the avant-garde Iris Clert gallery in posh Faubourg Saint Honoré. The models were exhibited on wooden mannequins in front of complementary modern paintings. Rabanne's garment projects were the talk of Paris. In 1966, Couturier Phillipe Venet used Rabanne's polychromatic plastic triangles for an evening coat in his collection. Rabanne's own business was now devouring 30,000 meter-square sheets of Rhodoid plastic a month. At the end of October, he opened his own boutique on the Rue Bergère, promising it would be "very dark inside with flourescent furniture . . . the light will come from the furniture."

Having exhausted the possibilities of plastic, Rabanne began constructing contemporary chain mail using tiny triangles of aluminum and leather cobbled together with flexible wire rings. He displayed his metal-and-leather blousons and leather miniskirts accompanied by a René Koernig soundtrack of whistles, dripping water, and percussion. Soon Rabanne was experimenting with one-piece, seamless molded plastic garments he produced in tandem with a line of premolded furniture. "Please don't call me a couturier," Rabanne requested. "I am an artisan."

In the space of a few years, the couture was forced between a Scylla and Charybdis of obsolescence and derivation. It was clear that, to ensure its surival, the couture was gradually revising its ground rules to accommodate a changing society. Vittorio Azario, chief of the giant couture fabric supplier Nattier Bros., said in 1967: "I frankly consider that high fashion is really deluxe ready-to-wear. Everything today is based on practicality." However, when the couture paraphrased ready-to-wear too faithfully, it was condemned as parasitical. When vinyl swept through the couture in January 1966, American designers took up the cudgels against what they perceived as a depredation. "You could have bought these things up at Paraphernalia months ago at $35 each. . . . It proves that there is no longer a need for couture," Paraphernalia's Joel Schumacher denounced. "It's as though they all just woke up and saw the world passing them by," the boutique's Deanna Littel snickered.

"Maison de Couture is turning into Laboratoire de Prêt-à-Porter," *WWD* noted in 1966. "These rtw [ready-to-wear] roughnecks like it or not have broken down the couture stockades from the outside." By January 1967, the couture found itself embattled, under siege from within and without. *Time* reported on "the sense of crisis" pervasive backstage during the January 1967 couture parades. In an age when the couture was generally acknowledged to

Pierre Cardin black silk crêpe sheath with multicolored pieces of plastic, shown in his spring 1968 couture collection

be derivative, the industry's governing body, the Chambre Syndicale de la Couture, was still going through the motions of protecting their constituency from plagiarism by controlling publicity-release dates. Before the January 1967 shows began, three couturiers had been expelled and two suspended by the Chambre Syndicale because they had issued photos in advance of dates established by that body. Pierre Cardin defended the early releases: "The couturier who has chosen to dress millions of women rather than five thousand ladies scattered round the world needs to have his collection talked about in order to support his ready-to-wear line."

Baffled and enraged, couture's *ancien régime* felt the ground crumbling underneath it. "The street is so vulgar it is like one huge derailment," fulminated Mme. Grès, whose Grecian draped jerseys had been a ravishing totem of *haute société* for thirty years. She decried "a class following fashion who did not use to," who "look at shop windows, not in magazines with haute couture models." The result? "Disaster." Balenciaga's reaction to the tumult outside his cloister walls was reported by *WWD* in 1966: "The Master thinks everyone has gone crazy." Buyer attendance kept slipping as epitaphs for the couture were sounded with increasing frequency. Midway through the January 1968 collections, Gloria Emerson professed in the *Times* that, while there were "hundreds of pretty ways to look in Paris this week . . . dozens and dozens of lovely dresses," it was nonetheless "difficult, even for the French, to keep up the old and precious pretense that Paris still dictates what women will wear. It is not even certain . . . that what Paris likes and Paris says will make any difference."

The couturiers began to flirt lightly with the American hippie culture soon after it reached Europe—although another year would pass before they mined the rich lode of ornamentation and folklore the hippies had revealed. Marc Bohan, who had earlier incorporated African, Asian Indian, and Russian iconography, revealed during his January 1968 collection that "deep inside him is a tiny hippie demanding to get out," according to Emerson. Bohan used amber, turquoise, and emerald jewelry; about his Indian-style necklaces, Emerson quipped: "They would love them in Haight-Ashbury too." But Bohan was still clinging to the traditional prerog-

After Natalie Wood went on a spree at Pierre Cardin's Paris couture salon, the house presented her with this sequinned evening dress. She gave it to her friend, model Peggy Moffitt, who accessorized it "as if it were a two-pound dress from Biba."

atives of high fashion; shortly before this collection, he sermonized: "We must get women to pull in their waists again. They are so used to being comfortable in loose dresses it will be difficult. But it must happen."

The Paris uprising of May 1968 was a paroxysm the couture could not ignore—if only because of its economic ramifications. Business at Dior, for example, plummetted by 67 percent that epochal month. Just as traumatic for the couture was Balenciaga's announcement, also in May, that his house would close. For years he had vowed regularly at collection time that his latest presentation would be the final one; the student insurrections were finally the *coup de grâce*. The grandee who only a few years before had seemed a demigod was now an anachronism. *WWD*'s eulogy was needlessly dismissive, reflecting a long-standing feud with the designer. Nevertheless its words contained some home truths. "Balenciaga's great contribution to fashion was that he knew how to streamline women of a certain age. But when a younger woman got into his clothes she looked dowdy. In later years, Balenciaga's clothes were too reserved, too studied, too middle-aging and too constructed for young people."

The spring conflagrations unleashed a storm of left wing sentiments from the young lions of the couture. "Let's kill the Couture," Emanuel Ungaro suggested, "kill it in the sense of the way it is now." Saint Laurent seized the new tide at its flood. "My small job as a couturier is to make clothes that reflect our times. . . . Recent political events, the reaction of young people to fashion and the way of life today make the Haute Couture a relic of the past. . . . I do not want to find myself in the past . . . or in a stronghold cut off from everything."

Yves Saint Laurent in 1969, outside his Rive Gauche boutique in London

The fall collection Saint Laurent presented in July 1968 was the couture's most overt expression of sympathy with the rioting legions of the previous May. Saint Laurent advocated somber pants for day and evening, strictly cut in dark hues but softened by a generous embellishment of hippie fringe. Conservative collections, too, reflected the proletarian tenor of the times. Dior's July défilé paraded fashions "fraught with the new social consciousness," Eugenia Sheppard reported, "mixed with enough brocade, rhinestones and ostrich to keep the non-thinking customers happy." Yet frippery and ostentation were momentarily in the doghouse. Private clients bemoaned the absence of resplendent ball gowns. It was the most seditious and populist moment in the couture of this century—as aberrational as the political climate itself. "The only remaining step, it seemed," reported *Newsweek*, "was the development of a tear-gas-proof mascara."

NEW YORK

In the eye of one of the most congested commercial districts of New York stood the magnificent Edwardian mansion that became, in the early 1960s, the headquarters of hairdresser Kenneth Battelle. The Beaux-Arts town house on 54th Street just east of Fifth Avenue had once been surrounded by residences of comparable splendor constructed by magnates of commerce at the turn of the century. The limestone facade of Battelle's stronghold—identified by his professional moniker "Kenneth"—was now enveloped by nondescript office towers built in the years following World War II. It was an incongruous beacon broadcast from a New York so remote it might never have existed.

Yet, undoubtedly, there were women among the moneyed and elegant flocking to Kenneth's whose grandmothers had danced quadrilles fifty years earlier in the rooms of that very town house. Donning pastel smocks—onto which some clipped the diamond brooches they wore to the salon—their hair was coiffed to the windblown configurations of the lion's mane style for which Kenneth's was famous. Like their grandmothers—the "Dollar Princesses" whose fortunes were exchanged for the status offered by impecunious scions of the English peerage—these women craved legitimation. When the great English couturiere Lucille established a New York beachhead in 1909, her American backers had informed her that it was her marital status as Lady Cosmo Duff-Gordon as much as, if not more than, her professional reputation that would insure a rousing success in the New World. A half century later, the women who crowded Kenneth's were visiting a shrine anointed by one of the nation's uncrowned royalty: Kenneth was the preferred hairdresser of Jacqueline Kennedy.

There was no more obvious manifestation of New York's innate diffidence in the delicate area of taste than the humility with which the New York fashion industry bowed to the dictates of the Paris haute couture. As the '60s began, New York was gazing no less adoringly at the French citadel of high fashion than it had been for almost a century. The American fashion industry had enjoyed a tremendous boom during World War II, when communication with the hibernating couture was interrupted. But in the years following Dior's cataclysmic "New Look" in 1947, the sovereignty of Paris again emerged unquestioned.

The kingpins of Seventh Avenue had once made deluxe pilgrimages to Paris via luxury liner. "Many well remember the midnight sailings [and] the shipside parties," journalist Rob Riley noted in 1967, evoking days when the *Ile-de-France* was nicknamed the "Seventh Avenue Special." Into the 1950s, retailer Hattie Carnegie customarily harvested up to two hundred ensembles at each of the Paris showings, out of which she reconstituted composite models for her ready-to-wear and made-to-order salons.

Maude Adams in coordinated corrugation from Giorgio Sant' Angelo

71

New York taking off: fashion model Birgitta Sayn-Wittgenstein in a herringbone suit with matching leggings

At the dawn of the '60s, virtually every designer in New York sought—in varying degrees—inspiration and validation in Paris. There were also many New York outlets for faithful replicas of couture prototypes. Bergdorf Goodman's Ethel Frankau's twice-yearly pilgrimages to Paris had begun in 1915 and continued until her retirement in 1967. The models she selected were copied meticulously, in the original fabrics, to the personalized measurements of the store's carriage-trade customers. At 57th Street's exclusive atelier Chez Ninon, couture designs were imported with the tastes of specific customers in mind.

Low-margin department stores Ohrbach's and Alexander's garnered reams of publicity from their seasonal recapitulation of ideas gestated by Paris. At biannual fashion shows staged by the department stores, couture originals paraded in tandem with their line-for-line copies. The attendance of celebrities and society women was ardently wooed by the two rival stores. Ohrbach's and Alexander's couture drive was their one bid for the patronage of the carriage trade, bestowing a patina of smart gentility upon their more generally plebian character.

"It's hard for people even to understand today," recalls New York sportswear designer Stan Herman, "how much New York was still under the influence of the couture. I remember in 1968 I came up with a collection of tunic dresses over pants, inspired by a group of Indian dolls Kezia Keeble [fashion editor at *Glamour* and *Vogue*] had told me about. I called Mildred

The buttoned-down early '60s in New York: fashions from Saks Fifth Avenue

72

Custin [then president of Bonwit Teller's] and told her she should see it. She laughed, but told me, 'Well, I'll look.' I chucked everything up to her. She sat in her big office and said 'No way. It's not going to work. They'll never let women into restaurants wearing these.'

"A month later I got a call from Mildred in Paris. St. Laurent had just done the same thing. She was going to reserve all the front windows at Bonwit's for my pants collection."

The New York fashion world revered Norman Norell, whose suave designs belied the hurly-burly that daily passed beneath his showroom at 550 Seventh Avenue, the garment district's most prestigious office tower. From early in his childhood in turn-of-the-century Indianapolis, Norell spent more hours in the audience of touring Broadway shows than he did in school. Years later, his black-tie openings approximated the festivity of an opening night on Broadway. Curtain time was 9:00 P.M., and midway through the showings those gathered adjourned for an "intermission" to gossip and sip champagne before Norell unveiled his evening wear.

Well-heeled and exuberant, Norell's audiences did not anticipate the epiphanies and radical fluctuations of the Paris couture. They looked forward to seeing a smoothly centrist product and a gently modulated yearly evolution that reaped plump dividends for the specialty stores that stocked the master's clothes. For Norell, women could "never be too simple during the day or too elaborate at night." His clothes combined the volumetric contours of Parisian couture at its more sculptured with the ease and simplicity of American sportswear. His perennial inclusion of wool jersey dresses in classic chemise shapes recalled his bond with Claire McCardell. The career of the American sportswear matriarch had developed parallel to Norell's as the dean of the elite market until her death in 1958. When Norell received the first Coty Award in 1943, he protested that its rightful recipient was McCardell.

The construction of Norell's clothes conformed to the architectural principles established by Paris couture of the Balenciaga school. His fabrics were reinforced with a stiff woven interfacing stitched into the fabric as it was smoothed over the round of the tailor's hand, guaranteeing a free-standing autonomy in the shapes and an extra lift to the rolled collars and hems.

During the '20s he had designed costumes for Gloria Swanson and Rudolph Valentino at the Paramount Studios in Astoria, New York, and for Broadway revues. Into the 1970s, Norell's most famous dresses recalled that long-ago New York—the giddy heyday of the Ziegfeld's Follies. Norell's hallmark "mermaid" sheaths were completely paved in sequins and were paraded by models sporting the kohl-darkened eyes of music-hall *vivandières* in the paintings of Kees van Dongen.

Cloak and daggery for the junior fashion market

"Where are the white gloves?" asked Kathleen Casey, editor-in-chief of *Glamour*. It was 1964, and rookie editor Kezia Keeble was consistently omitting them from the photographic sessions she supervised. "I was too young to know never to use oneself as an example to prove a point," recalls Keeble, today a partner in the public relations firm Keeble, Cavaco, and Duka. "So I went ahead and told her that many women had stopped wearing them to work. I myself never wore them any more. 'Then you're not a lady,' she told me."

In its punctilious concern with correctness, New York looked to made-to-order monarch Main Rousseau Bocher—whose professional sobriquet fused into "Mainbocher"—as a lodestar. Born in Chicago to parents of Scottish descent, Mainbocher nurtured a strong strain of Calvinist prudence expressed not only in his character, but in his designs as well. His aesthetic pivoted, as did Chanel's, on the inverse snobbery of rich women wearing phenomenally expensive and luxurious clothes that evinced a subdued, seemingly austere simplicity. Implicit in his output was the retaliation of old money against nouveau-riche ostentation. Mainbocher's cre-

75

Celebrants at a loft party given by fashion photographer Jerry Schatzburg in 1965

ations were explicitly designed for a select consumer. Exquisite dressmaker details executed with "loving hands" finesse were visible only to the spectator sufficiently privileged to see them at close range.

During the 1930s, Mainbocher had become the only American to penetrate the xenophobic bastion of the Paris haute couture, until Hitler's invasion forced his return to the U.S. Many described Mainbocher as a throwback to one of Henry James's disenchanted exiles, but Mainbocher's designs found inspiration in their creator's heartland heritage. He burrowed into native Americana, championing crisp gingams, organdies, and cotton piques, and dresses quaintly overlaid with apronlike panels.

During the 1960s, Seventh Avenue believed devoutly in dues-paying. It was enthralled by the many Horatio Alger stories of penniless immigrants who had arduously climbed to the top of the industry. Hattie Carnegie, one of the pluckiest, had entered the business as a fifteen-year-old delivery girl in 1904. By the time she died fifty years later, Carnegie owned a private house on Fifth Avenue and included most of her family on her company's payroll. Norell, sixty years old as the '60s began, was entering the peak half-decade of his career. So was Ben Zuckerman, who had begun his business in 1911. Seventh Avenue traditionally attached no credence to the whims of callow youth. It demanded that even designers of clothes for teenagers be themselves seasoned veterans.

For a fledgling or an outsider, Seventh Avenue could seem like a barred fortress. Betsey Johnson, working as an editorial assistant at *Mademoiselle* after graduating from Syracuse University with an art degree, began her designing career selling homemade sweaters to her colleagues. "I realized I liked making clothes better than drawing clothes, but I couldn't get an interview anywhere," Johnson remembers. "With no credits in design, I couldn't get past the receptionist's secretary."

Yet even within the mainstream of the Seventh Avenue establishment, the agitation of the rebels across the Atlantic began to register seismographically. A special Coty Award was presented in 1965 to a group of young designers fielding the junior market—Sylvia de Gay, Stan Herman, Edie Gladstone, Victor Joris, Gayle Kirkpatrick, Deanna Littell, Leo Narducci, Don Simonelli, and Bill Smith. "The new doyennes of fashion," wrote Gloria Steinem in the *New York Times* in January 1965, "don't follow Diana Vreeland; Diana Vreeland follows them." When Vreeland had hired Caterine Milinare two years earlier, she had specifically designated Milinaire as *Vogue*'s pipeline to the world of youthful fashion. Milinaire was instructed to scout the by-ways on and off Seventh Avenue, and the graduating classes of design acad-

(LEFT) Warhol "Superstar" International Velvet. (ABOVE)
Warhol adjutant Gerard Malanga, in flowered shirt,
behind the girl in the striped suit.

77

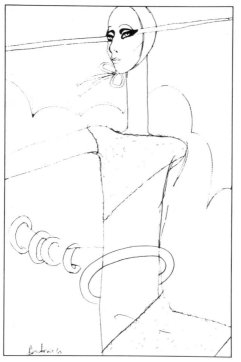

Antonio Lopez sketch of bouclé knit dress with fluorescent tubes by Ingeborg Marcus, 1965

Low-heeled shoes supplanted the spindly stillettos of the '50s, and design interest shifted from the heel to the throat and toe.

emies. She was to search for the young Turks Vreeland anticipated would arise in response to the new ready-to-wear stars of London and Paris.

In September 1965, the boutique Paraphernalia opened on Madison Avenue between 66th and 67th streets. A laboratory and showcase for untried design talent, Paraphernalia heralded a new epoch in fashionable New York.

"Personally, I've always thought anybody who takes fashion seriously is ridiculous. I mean they're just clothes. Therefore they should be fun, and nothing about wearing them should be taken seriously." This is the credo of Paul Young, merchandizing wizard of Pop Fashion in New York during the mid '60s. Young's founding of Paraphernalia was the culmination of a half-decade he had spent marketing avant-garde European fashion. His coup in leading the

Paraphernalia's London look, photographed in Central Park, 1965

J. C. Penney chain from a rear-guard to a navigatory presence in the young fashion market reached Karl Rosen, president and founder of Puritan, a mass manufacturer concentrating on half-size women's dresses. Rosen asked Young to steer Puritan to a position of strength in the youth market. Young subsequently initiated "Youthquake," a Puritan division manufacturing collections designed by the new crop of European ready-to-wear stars. "I told Karl I'd only come to Puritan if he agreed to launch Paraphernalia. 'It'll be a stage for young designers. We can pick up actual retail results and show the buyers that these styles *are* wanted by the consumer.'"

Young selected a motley group for Paraphernalia's charter design team. Autodidact Betsey Johnson was recommended to Young by *Mademoiselle* editors Noni Moore and Sande Horvitz. Deanna Littell had graduated from Parsons in 1960, when her valedictory design won her the Norell thimble award as well as coverage in *Life* magazine. She was included in the special collective Coty citation. Heaped with laurels, Carol Friedland and Joel Schumacher also had recently graduated from Parsons. "I feel that young talent is often sabotaged on Seventh Avenue," Young avowed shortly before the store opened. His designers leapfrogged to an immediate position of autonomy. "Straight out of school, we were set up in our own workrooms," recalls Carol Friedland. "I was told to do eight pieces for the opening of the store—they could be whatever I wanted." The common motivation of the designers was "to do something interesting and creative and different, and make your statement," recalls Winkie Donovan, a popular model who often participated in the store's runway shows. "We were all protesting one way or the other."

During the 1960s, New York witnessed a significant rapprochement between the worlds of fashion and fine art. The cross-pollination recalled the hothouse atmosphere of Paris between the wars. Parisian gallery openings had then been a prime arena for fashions that were often inspired by the same Zeitgeist as the art their wearers were observing. In the 1960s the phenomenon repeated itself: "It's called opening night at an exhibit of New Art, but the objective is to get as much attention as possible by wearing the wildest thing," *WWD* noted in January 1967.

Perhaps the one true symbiosis between fine art and high fashion had crystallized during the 1920s in the work of artist/designer Sonia Delauney. Delauney's textile and fashion designs echoed the refracted color abstractions she produced on canvas. During the '30s, Elsa Schiaparelli's designs had incorporated the perverse disjunctions of Surrealism. Schiaparelli also commissioned personal friends and princes of the Surrealist movement to execute fabric

New York socialites in Pop Art dresses, 1964

and accessory designs. Cocteau had limned a Greek maenad's flowing mane in glass beads across the sleeve of a linen suit. Dali's lobster-spattered print was made into an organza evening dress; the pockets of a Schiaparelli suit were trimmed with leather insignias describing Surrealism's ubiquitous pair of ripe red lips.

During the '60s, New York observed a more rigidly stratified hierarchy. A greater cleft was hewn between fine and applied artists than had prevailed during the utopia-planning of the '20s and the casual oxymorons of the '30s. Pop Art's debt to mass commercial culture initially had been a thorn in the side of artists lobbying for serious academic affirmation. New York's fine arts community had been chastized during the '60s for elevating Pop Art to a high art orthodoxy. Somewhat defensively, then, New York's fine art oligarchy did not encourage the redistribution of the imagery of contemporary art back to its commercial sources.

While the collaborations of the '20s and '30s were rarely repeated, the new art of the '60s nonetheless supplied a fertile lode of invention for the decade's fashion designers. In the fall of 1964, Larry Aldrich, a leading Seventh Avenue manufacturer, commissioned a collection of fabrics inspired by his extensive collection of Op Art paintings. Aldrich's gesture sparked a rage for garments hosting these oscillating spatial conundrums. At the opening of a Museum of Modern Art Op survey in spring 1965, the dresses of many of the observers mirrored the kinetic geometries displayed on the walls of the gallery. "Many of the previewers seemed as bent as the artists on manipulating the wandering eye," reported *Time* magazine. That same year, Marion Javits approached Paul Young about starting a Puritan division to retail textile designs by Robert Rauschenberg, Larry Rivers, and several others in the pantheon of contemporary American artists. Although Young was interested, the idea did not get past the discussion stage.

Fortrel dress by Deanna Littell for Mam'selle Boutique in 1967

John Kloss, a consistently inventive designer during the '60s, had fraternized with many then-unknown Pop and Minimalist artists when Kloss and artist Robert Indiana both inhabited lofts in the same Coenties Slip building in Lower Manhattan. Kloss produced color-field dresses "two years before Yves Saint Laurent," reported the *New York Times* when the Paris designer's famous Mondrianesque collection appeared. For his first Paraphernalia collection, Joel Schumacher designed an A-line jersey dress aping Indiana's famous "L-O-V-E" emblem. Schumacher's letters were stenciled in orange over a green jersey body, the void of the "O" cut out over the wearer's navel.

Paraphernalia's outré wares resonated with echoes from Pop Art's distant antecedents in the subversive ethics of the dada and Futurist movements. Dresses at Paraphernalia became found objects fashioned from industrial materials previously consigned to utilitarian purposes.

Paraphernalia's brave new world embraced fabrics "you'd spray with Windex, rather than dry-clean," recalls Betsey Johnson. "We were into plastic flash synthetics that looked like synthetics. It was: 'Hey, your dress looks like my shower curtain!' The newer it was, the weirder—the better."

Johnson arrived at Paraphernalia with her interest in unorthodox raw materials already piqued. Joining *Mademoiselle* as a guest college editor in 1964, she was dispatched as assis-

*John Kloss crêpe dress and matching lingerie,
photographed in 1966 in the designer's apartment
before a canvas by his friend Robert Indiana*

tant to the fabric editor: "My editor was about eleven months pregnant, so I had to cover the market. I had to redo her files, and D. J. White has got to be one of the most creative fabric women in the industry." Johnson's future designs benefited from her review of dossiers recording an incredible gamut: "what the industrial people used, stuff they were making car interiors out of, fabrics they were lining caskets with, the materials with which they were insulating spaceships." Once installed at Paraphernalia, Johnson became an inveterate husbander of untried goods. Studying sequins, she envisioned the metallic sheet fabric out of which they were stamped: "I finally wound up at 'Coating Products of New Jersey.'"

"Smart salesmen would realize we were these experimental kids and come to us with something new and funky," relates Deanna Littell. "Someone brought me a plastic, like a leather-ette, that was coated with a glow-in-the-dark film. It was used for policemen's night raincoats. They had started manufacturing it in day-glo purples and greens." Littell fashioned

Surrounded by sketches in her office at the Paraphernalia showroom, Betsey Johnson wears her tinsel motorcycle jacket in 1966.

a series of evening raincoats "in these florescent colors, but trimmed in the contrasting white bands which glowed at night," providing an incandescent coat that glowed round the clock.

As U.S. foreign policies increasingly polarized the '60s, employing the Stars and Stripes as apparel became a barbed critique. At the peak of Pop Fashion, however, co-opting the flag distilled a cooler, more ambiguous wit. Deanna Littell remembers locating a by-the-yard outlet for the printed bunting out of which pint-sized five-and-ten-store flags are cut. Inspired by Jasper Johns's flag series, Littell devised a shirt accordingly blanketed with tiny flags, relieved by white collars and cuffs. "Paul Young thought it was fabulous. We planned spectacular Fourth of July windows," Littell recalls. Paraphernalia learned, however, that the Daughters of the American Revolution was bringing suit against another manufacturer for another contravention, and was vigilantly monitoring similar defilements. "I thought it would have been fun —part of the whole spirit—to indeed have the shop closed down by the DAR," remembers

Deanna Littell, model Jenny Garrigues in Littell's trapunto tunic and matching boots, John Kloss, and Geraldine Stutz—then president of Henri Bendel— 1967. Kloss and Littell were designing for Bendel's "Studio."

Betsey Johnson in 1968, wearing a jumpsuit made from the football jerseys of then-husband John Cale, guitarist with the Velvet Underground

Littell. "But Paul felt that while, yes, we were on the cutting edge, we'd do better to keep the store open."

For evening, Paraphernalia proposed translucent slip dresses that suggested skeins of cellophane, designed to be worn over flesh-colored, bias-cut satin body-stockings. Johnson ransacked motorcycle supply stores for hardware fittings, trimming black-leather A-line mini-dresses with grommets. She etched an X-ray illusion onto one collection of dresses by outlining in silver the armature of the skeleton at the collarbone, pelvis, and arms.

The prominence of silver in Warhol's spectrum contributed to its importance in the palette of Pop Fashion. Silver evoked the tinsel glitter of nighttime hedonism, the ubiquitous chrome of postindustrial society, and the futuristic sheen of vehicles for outer-space exploration. Immediately identified by her aluminum foil tank dresses, Johnson was approached by Warhol adjutant Gerard Malanga to dress Warhol's acolytes for a magazine portrait of the artist and his entourage. At the sitting, she met Warhol "Superstar" Edie Sedgwick, whose peculiar glamour—that of a waif on the razor's edge—provided a perfect vehicle for Johnson's most extreme designs. Sedgwick became Johnson's fitting model, and Johnson subsequently designed Sedgwick's state-of-the-art wardrobe for her aborted 1967 film *Ciao Manhattan*.

Many of Paraphernalia's designs echoed the lineaments of "auto-mate"—moving art installations that integrated the machinery of daily life into the clinical detachment of the gallery setting. A pop fashion dress became a multipart object in flux. Detachable sleeves could be zipped on or off. Johnson designed a vinyl dress that was sold with an accompanying kit of adhesive foil scallops. They could be adhered and recombined in endless permutations.

Dresses celebrated process, becoming ambulatory demonstrations of performance art. Johnson recalls a *pièce d'occasion* made from a fad paper, "the kind you watered and it grew herbs. It was amazing. There were little seeds planted in a kind of blotter paper, very soft—

Lauren Hutton wearing Betsey Johnson's plastic slip dress with do-it-yourself appendages made from sequin sheeting. Shoes by Herbert Levine.

kind of like a Handi-Wipe. It was like those Magic Rocks you put in water. When you watered the dress, it grew these strange little blossoms." Johnson's concoction fell into the Paraphernalia genus of throwaways meant to last one night.

While Paraphernalia's designers had their fingers pressed to the pulse of pop outrage, their work also manifested an allegiance to the American sportswear tradition embodied by pioneers Claire McCardell, Anne Klein, and Bonnie Cashin. Johnson names the dance recital costumes she wore in elementary school as a major inspiration for her work at Paraphernalia: "Those tricky little numbers had to perform on your body or you were in trouble. I always wanted my clothes to move on the body, to be as much an extension of the body as a leotard." In high school, Johnson ran her own dance school, making regular trips to Manhattan from her home in suburban Connecticut to order fabric for her students' recital costumes. "In high school I got to know a huge range of wonderful stretchy satins and Helenka jerseys. And, sure enough, at Paraphernalia when I wanted those same kinds of fabrics I knew just where to go."

The New York establishment sold luxurious clothes that telegraphed the wearer's wealth and discernment—"Social Security for the Rich," as the *New York Times* termed Norell's clothes in 1966. Paraphernalia sold arresting, sometimes unprecedented clothes that promised the wearer inclusion in a coterie of the initiated. *Chic* was the laudatory buzzword of the New York Establishment. Paraphernalia's clothes, on the other hand, were *in*.

Paraphernalia's cachet was bestowed for an investment infinitely less than that exacted by the New York couture. The least expensive Norell dress was $500; the low end of Mainbocher's collections grazed the four-figure threshold. Most of Paraphernalia's separates, however, retailed for less than $50.

New York's fashionable young population was increasingly unwilling to invest in expensive clothes, no matter how economically their cost was eventually amortized. Victor Joris told the *New York Times* after his Coty citation in 1965: "People will spend $100 for an outfit they will wear for a year. Next year, they will be going new places, doing new dances—they will want new clothes."

The expected lifespan of many of Paraphernalia's designs was considerably briefer. "People would walk into the store dressed in their straight clothes," recalls Paul Young. "They'd buy something and put it on. Then and there they'd apply an outrageous make-up, before heading directly to a party. They were buying something to wear tonight and more or less throw away tomorrow. We priced our clothes with that in mind."

Paraphernalia's operational procedures themselves subscribed to Pop Art's glorification of the fleeting moment. New merchandise appeared—and just as quickly vanished irrevocably—on a weekly, even daily basis. Durability was, therefore, hardly the criterion by which Paraperhnalia's following assessed its clothes. "Our standard eventually became pretty good," says Paul Young, but it was at first "terrible." That mattered not a whit to customers intent on riding the crest of the wave-of-the-moment. Demand for Betsey Johnson's famous "Julie Christie dress" voraciously exceeded supply. A cotton-knit shirtdress with drooping white "Beatles" collar and turned-back cuffs, the mini-dress was given this eponymous shorthand after the actress chose it for a *Mademoiselle* photo shoot.

"Usually we began with a lot of twelve or twenty-four of a number for one store," recalls Paul Young. "But I liked this dress so much I ordered forty-eight. And then the entire stock sold out the first day in the store. But we held on to about half a dozen where the seams were coming apart. We hadn't realized how much seam allowance you need in a fitted dress. It was late one Saturday, and I was at the store waiting on a customer myself. She wanted this dress *badly*. 'The seams are coming apart,' I told her. 'It doesn't matter,' she replied. 'I can't give you any reduction,' I impressed upon her. 'It doesn't matter,' she said. 'I'll take it. I'll sew it up myself!'"

"If a dress is sold out today," says Betsey Johnson, "you can get a knock-off: you can get it somewhere else. It is *nothing* like it was then. I felt the customers at Paraphernalia were looking to our clothes as passports to a new age, a new birth."

The look of Paraphernalia consummated the wedding of fashion and art that the store celebrated. Many commented that Paraphernalia resembled an art gallery more than a conventional retail space. Its ambience was minimalist. Streaked in white, silver, and neutral-colored wood, the store was masterminded by architect Ulrich Franzen. Emboldened by the enthusiasm of Paraphernalia's steering committee and the store's "progressive, timely aura," Franzen made a unique digression into retail design. He conceived of the store as "a continuous Happening." Two brownstone fronts were combined into a common facade curtained by a double-height glass window. The store was landscaped with a series of small stages, on which a live model frugged at peak hours in the most sensational Paraphernalia dress of the moment. Silver devices poured theatrical lighting upon these plinths. "You never saw a lot of merchandise," explains Franzen. "From the street all that was visible was the one or two designs in action on the live model, and the people at the back of the store." Selling was done only on the second floor, but the sales desk was situated at the rear of the first story. "I don't know if these were customers," estimates Franzen, "but there was always a crowd looking in at the storefront." Franzen stocked Paraphernalia's sleek interior with specially designed tractor seats that were later exhibited at the Whitney Museum and abroad.

In 1968, Franzen's penultimate Paraphernalia embodied a concept that remains novel to this day. Located on the northeast corner of Lexington Avenue and 55th Street, the store conformed to the genre then termed "Electrographic Architecture." Across the front of the store, the legend "Paraphernalia" was etched in neon, the letters pursued by a chase sequence that washed them canonically from white to red. The store was kept pitch black at all times of day. Tucked inside round aluminum enclosures, no clothes were visible to the shopper. The customer was instead issued a remote-control device that allowed her to project at her discretion a video résumé of the items for sale on large screens at the back of the store. When she chose an article to try on, a salesperson would give the customer the garment and direct her to a dressing room.

From its inception, Paraphernalia galvanized the celebrities of the new millennium. "Paul had the ability," avows Betsey Johnson, "to fascinate the rich and powerful as easily as he charmed the naive and vulnerable kid I was." Young insured the continued attention and support of the country's most celebrated family by choosing Susan Burden, a college roommate of Joan Kennedy, as PR director. Young became a conduit between the store and a vast network of celebrities who were also personal friends. They contributed invaluable promotional support to his brainchild.

Lexington Avenue Paraphernalia, opened in 1968

Live model in the window of the Greenwich Village Paraphernalia

"Paraphernalia is the center of the fashion target for the young," reported the *New York Times* one month after the pilot store opened. The hip offspring of liberal East Coast dynasties were as susceptible as any to the lure of the boutique. "Marietta Tree called me up one day and asked if she could bring her daughter Penelope along," recalls Paul Young. "She was taking her to Truman Capote's party at the Plaza, but she didn't want to wear anything *too* formal. So I introduced Penelope to Betsey Johnson. Betsey devised a fantastic fluorescent lime-green dress." A bodice of two triangles of matte jersey floating above a floor-length skirt, Johnson's design was a witty exercise in sleight-of-hand. When Tree stood still, her gown resembled a columnar creation of Mme. Grès in Paris. Directly she hit the dance floor, her dress billowed away, revealing that it was instead floating panels cut to the midriff. "Penelope was the hit of the party," recalls Young. "Everyone else was overdressed in stiff ball gowns and bouffants."

"All of us at Paraphernalia were kind of in competition with one another," recalls Elisa Stone. "We were friendly, we smiled and said 'Hello,' but we really didn't comingle. I was determined to make my stuff different from *anything*, *anywhere*. But the competition was good-natured. It was not killer rivalry." Stone became renowned for her mastery of that most iconically ephemeral '60s pop fashion—paper dresses. After graduating from UCLA with an art degree, Stone had designed custom-made precious jewelry in Beverly Hills, and had authored a sportswear line for a West Coast manufacturer. Nonetheless, upon her arrival in New York in 1965, "people told me I couldn't do anything because I was from LA and hadn't gone to Parsons," Stone recalls. By day Stone supported herself as a bookkeeper; by night, she constructed dresses like silhouetted paper cutouts, "just for the fun of it. I thought maybe I could some time show them to someone." Model Gretchen Regan arranged an introduction to Paul Young. "Paraphernalia was the perfect climate for me."

Stone's preferred medium was a porous but firm weave with a pebbly texture resembling the surface of a paper towel. "I built them like real A-line dresses. I would sew the shoulders and the side seam, sew the backseam and then use Velcro to hold it in the back." Onto her paper chemises Stone affixed streamers of heavier constructionlike paper, from which paper cubes sometimes dangled. Stone would use scissors to flute the pendulous paper strips. "I wanted everything to move."

"I loved the idea that my clothes were not going to last. I thought of them as toys." Stone's dollhouse workshop reached its apotheosis when a dress she had made out of a transparent theatrical lighting gel was shown on the cover of the August 1967 *Harper's Bazaar*. "The gel only comes twenty inches by twenty-four, so I was limited in what I could do. I put a

Elisa Stone dresses of paper and plastic

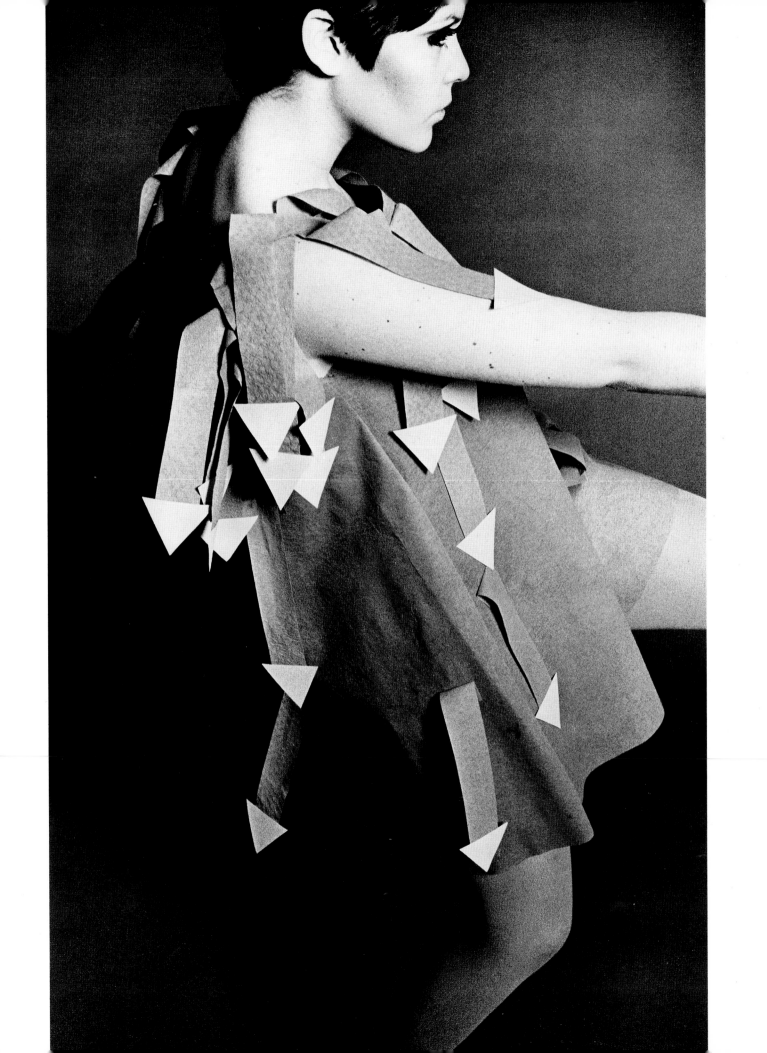

seam in the front and a seam in the back, with criss-cross straps at the neck." At the shoulders, Stone's *chef d'oeuvre* sprouted frills of the same gel, which she had fringed on a paper cutter.

"When I took the gelly dresses to Paraphernalia's shipping department, I packed them one on top of the other the way you would stack paper cups. As soon as I got there, they hung them on hangers in the stockroom. They looked just wonderful—like transparent candy." At Paraphernalia's Greenwich Village branch, Stone's dresses described a lambent rainbow against a snowy white ground. "Maybe eight or ten of them sat up on the wall, in the entire array of colors—orange and yellow, red and green. How I wish I'd taken a color photograph."

By 1966, twenty-four-year-old Betsey Johnson had emerged as New York's answer to the bellwethers of London and Paris ready-to-wear. The late Sally Kirkland, formerly *Life*'s fashion editor, recalled: "We had an exclusive contract to photograph Twiggy her first day in New York in 1967. But because she was such legitimate news by then, a rabble of newspaper guys were following us around, claiming she was public domain. And the one thing that Twiggy wanted to do in New York was meet Betsey Johnson. Paraphernalia was the first place she wanted to go. So up to Paraphernalia we trooped, surrounded by what looked like the entire New York press corps."

New York's old guard began to panic over the shock troops of Pop Fashion. "As amusing as slang fashion is, it is not a complete language," Mainbocher objected in the program notes to his spring 1967 showing. "I think women should dress as they talk: a basis of grammar, lightened here and there with a sprinkling of argot."

"As an American kid doing new fashion and doing what I wanted," recalls Betsey Johnson, "Marvin Israel and Diane Arbus invited me to talk to the fashion students at Parson's. I felt very strongly that the kids wanted to hear from me. I was dying to talk to them. But they couldn't get me through the system. Parson's wouldn't let me *near* that school."

The first fashions identified with New York's dance mania of in the '60s were the short cocktail sheaths worn at the Peppermint Lounge on West 45th Street very early in the decade. Armored in the hallowed chic of the Little Black Dress, soignée women descended upon this grungy but irresistible cradle of the Twist. Shorter and slimmer than the crinolined gowns in which the women attended formal dances, Twist dresses were usually made out of *peau de soie* or faille—a crisp fabric with a muted sheen.

By 1965, revelers were plundering thrift shops, having discovered—according to the *New York Times*—that "The flapper's slip of a dress has proved as functional for the frug as it was

The boutique at the Chelsea discotheque, 1966

for the Charleston." The body's gyrations were unconstricted in simple chemises and they were echoed by responsive cascades of fringe. By 1967, *le dernier cri* was sounded by anything short, sleek, and phosphorescent. Flaring body-skimmers banded with sequins, drenched in Fauvist prints or syncopated color zones were often slung from a harness ring. Glitter-flecked stockings were an inevitable accoutrement. Often, a swift little evening coat maintained a veneer of coordinated propriety. Norell's short fitted organza coat in the spring of 1967, emblazoned with Roman stripes, was one of the designer's most timely suggestions of the decade.

Café society watering holes of the '50s allowed admittance and dispensed preferential treatment according to the applicant's rank and wealth. Money and fame were as efficacious as calling cards in the '60s as they had ever been; they were now supplemented, however, by the more common currency of uniquely styled appearance. "Style is what you've got to have to get into Salvation," reported Chauncey Howell in *Holiday* magazine. By the time Salvation reigned in Greenwich Village late in the '60s, style ordained a uniquely fabricated appearance. "Come as a Regency fop, a restoration trull, or as a saffron-robed eunuch from the court of the Dowager Empress of China, and Mike [the club's sentinel] will certainly let you in."

Cheek by jowl with the wealthy acreage of Sutton Place, Le Club opened in 1963, duplicating the cushy ambience of London's semiprivate discotheques. It deployed red velvet walls and a darkened bar with velvet banquettes. A large club room with a marble mantlepiece and a two-story tapestry surmounted a balconied backgammon room and a small dance floor. Le Club was "full of very beautiful people," recalls designer Dory Coffee. "You saw lovely older women in real Chanel suits, as well as young models wearing something backless and risqué from Paraphernalia." Music was chicly foreign—bossa nova, Charles Aznavour, Mirielle Mathieu. Dancing was intimate and low-key.

While Le Club remains popular to this day, the *boîtes de nuit* that followed substituted raucous bedlam for its discreet enchantment. Sibyl Burton's Arthur's was the blueprint for a new breed of enormous dance-hall hangars, teeming with clamorous crowds cutting loose to the frenetic strains of electronic music.

By the time Cheetah opened near Times Square in April 1966, the discotheque had become a self-contained Aladdin's Cave, in which the visitor surrendered his or her everyday identity in search of Dionysian transport. Cheetah employed many conspiring elements to bedazzle its switched-on congregation. Banks of colored lights shone on its patrons. Suspended high above the writhing crowds, huge sheets of chrome—a giant mobile created by industrial designer Michael Lax—undulated rhythmically, while at the club's opening night the customers echoed the *mise en scène*: "each girl was more electric than the next," Eugenia Sheppard reported. "The swinging hair. The wild colors. The mini-mini skirts." At The World, in Garden City, Long Island, twenty-one screens simultaneously showed different film footage, creating a cinematic anarchy to parallel the live cacophony.

Inaugurated downtown, on Saint Mark's Place, in June of 1967, the Electric Circus became New York's ultimate mixed-media pleasure dome. Its hallucinogenic light baths enthralled every sector of New York society. "When you're finished with reality, come up here," invited Jerry Brandt, twenty-eight-year-old owner of the club. Borrowing further from

the West Coast culture, the Electric Circus was populated with the roustabouts of the annual "Renaissance Fairs" of San Francisco and Los Angeles. *Life* reported:

Magnified images of children in a park, a giant armadillo or Lyndon Johnson disport themselves on the white plastic sculptured expanse of the tentlike ceiling. Gigantic light-amoebae rove among the images, pulsating and contracting with the relentless beat of a rock band. . . . A young man with the moon and stars painted on his back soars overhead on a silver trapeze, and a ring juggler manipulates colored hoops amid shaggy hippies who unconcernedly perform a pagan tribal dance. . . . Stroboscopic lights flicker over the dancers, breaking up their move-ments into a jerky parody of an old-time Chaplin movie. But then, loud, loud the hippies' national anthem, the Beatles A Day in the Life, *begins, and there is stillness, reverie.*

Going gamely into the night, one now required clothes that were fantastic as well as stylish. The visitor dressed to interact or be integrated with the enveloping electronic environment. Deanna Littell remembers locating a fuchsia and white Buffalo-check fabric at a theatrical supply store. Littell devised a cowboy shirt designed to be worn with a fuchsia day-glow vinyl miniskirt. "Being theatrical fabric, the shirt reflected black light. I can still remember Marisa Berenson at one of the Paraphernalia parties. With the strobe light flashing, all you could see was the shirt."

Cheetah initiated a trend by selling earmarked discotheque attire in a boutique included in a multi-level complex consisting of dance floor, underground-film screening room, and hot-

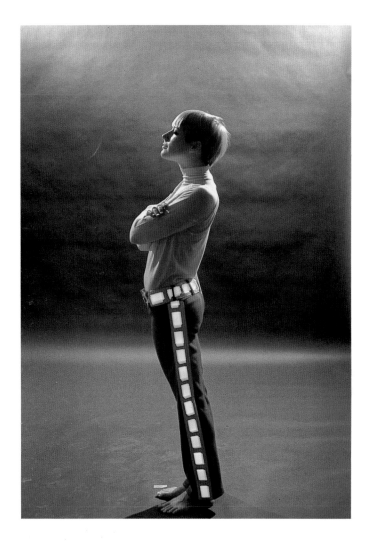

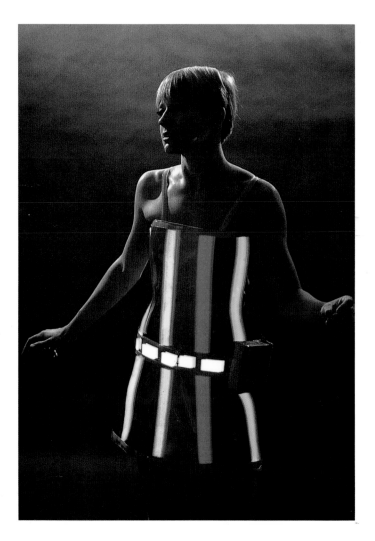

Diana Dew wearing her light-up dress and pants

dog stand. The proprietor of the Cheetah's boutique noticed that many customers were purchasing clothes to exchange for those they had arrived in, so the checkrooms were were specially expanded. At the Electric Circus, "Clothes, Furbelows, Feathers and Astonishments," were all purveyed. Salvation's "Stone the Crows" shop promised clothes that "Hobbits would just love to wear, if they could."

The quintessential interactive disco fashion was unveiled at Paraphernalia in the winter of 1966: a vinyl dress that self-illuminated at the command of the wearer. It was not the first time fashion had been wired for artifical light. Schiaparelli had come up with a handbag that lit up when snapped open. At her Teeney Weeny boutique on upper Madison Avenue, Joan "Tiger" Morse sold dresses seeded with miniature light bulbs. For his July 1966 hommage to Pop Art, Yves Saint Laurent created a bridal gown that flashed an incandescent flower, which enlivened the runway show's traditional finale.

Paraphernalia's light-up dress was the brainchild of electrical engineer Diana Dew. "Karl Rosen's brother Jerry found her up in Massachusetts," remembers Paul Young. "Jerry called me: 'She's absolutely someone you should meet. She's *your* type of person!' he laughed. Diana was the first woman I ever saw who painted her hair with streaks of color. Different colors every day."

Dew actualized an idea that had stayed largely within the conceptual realm by inventing a miniaturized power source potentiometer. Shrunk to the size of a cigarette pack, Dew's miniature battery pack fit on the belt of the dress and obviated the need for bulky power supply. The potentiometer regulated the frequency of the blinking hearts or stars, which could be co-ordinated to the throbbing beat of the disco soundtrack. "They're hyper-delic transsensory experiences," Dew boasted. Dew's innovation was later acquired by the U.S. military for ground-to-air signalling.

Retailing at $150, Dew's *pièce de résistance* was quite a bit more expensive than most of Paraphernalia's fare, although its price tag hovered just a hair above the cost price, claims Paul Young. About three hundred of the dresses were sold, calculates Frank Lo Pinto, Paraphernalia's production manager. "We didn't have a single return for mechanical failure," Paul Young boasts.

Spinning a mile a minute at discotheque blast-offs, hostess at saturnalian promotional events, Joan "Tiger" Morse was Pop Fashion's madcap mistress of ceremonies. This Perle Mesta of Pop New York first surfaced in the early '60s as a young matron running a boutique out of an apartment in a mansion on the Upper East Side. Morse circled the globe searching for rare and exotic fabrics. She turned her booty into unique creations for a cadre of wealthy

Manhattan collectors. As her business expanded into two floors of the town house, Morse began to load her premises with every variety of bibelot and bric-a-brac she had acquired on her voyages to the Orient, Africa, and the Middle East. Morse's store—A La Carte—was filled to bursting with *tchotchkes*. It was the blueprint for a series of retail spaces this Brooklyn robber baroness transformed into groaning storehouses.

Morse promiscuously championed exquisite hand embroidery and outrageous specimens of vernacular kitsch. She perfectly gauged the beat of this epoch when every canon of "good" taste was being pummeled. Everything that surrounded her was for sale, including the gumball machine prominently displayed in her high-rise apartment.

Morse was one of the decade's most bizarre and prescient self-styled fashion freaks. She was "a hard-boiled, very bright businesswoman," assesses illustrator Joe Eula, "who went all over the world and came back with Tiger Morse." Her appearance was an amalgam of an on-the-forefront Mod and a provincial Jewish mama. Her sunglasses "would have been the envy of any woman in Miami," Eula notes. "They had enough rhinestones and spikes going on to cover half a block." By contrast, her lips were glossed with frosted white salve—state of the art.

"I want to be where it's happening today and it's not in custom," Morse said in 1966. Late in 1964, she had christened an East 58th Street wholesale showroom "Kaleidoscope." In April 1965, Morse staged a tie-in to her new venture at the Greenross Gallery on East 57th Street. Described as a "Kaleidoscope of extravagant fashions and accessories," Morse's exhibit had been shown previously in Europe. Dressed in a bird-wing headdress and brocade boots, Morse called repeatedly for a phonograph during the visit of *New York Times* reporter Angela Taylor: "I can't work without my music," she explained, going into a few steps of the Boogaloo.

About this time, Morse visited Michael Mott's apartment to look over jewelry he had fashioned into mirrored cubes and rhinestone-studded orbs like golf balls. Donning her ubiquitous sunglasses, her tumble-down blonde mane flying, Morse was a hyperkinetic comet. "She paced around madly, shrieking over things she liked," recalls Mott.

To launch a wholesale collection in December 1965, Morse threw a party in a tapestry designer's loft on East 47th Street, to which what seemed like the entire fashion community of Manhattan flocked. "I'd been to quite a few loft parties by then, but never one as crazy as this," recalls Mott. "It was indescribable. The chaos. The clothes. I remember Veruschka wearing something very bare. But Tiger was by far the the most insane thing there."

The lights dimmed to pitch blackness in the overcrowded loft, which vibrated with the reverberations of electronic amplification and undulating hoards. Pinpointed by spotlights, Morse appeared, tricked out in silver foil, frugging with her models on catwalks slung precariously above the melée.

A genius at self-promotion, Morse was a nightbird with distinctly raffish tastes. Invariably ferried by limousine, she made nightly gravitations to the kookiest, most venturesome nerve centers of the city. Eula remembers Morse arriving at a Metropolitan Museum party "all lit up, strapped with batteries from her shoes to her sunglasses."

Morse's social pedigree—her father was a noted architect—and her impressive if unauthenticated academic credentials—she claimed graduate study in art history—also enticed more staid elements of the New York retailing class. In the spring of 1966, Andrew Goodman, owner and president of Bergdorf Goodman, demonstrated his commitment by devoting the store's Fifth Avenue display windows to a series of tableaus in which Morse's vinyl dresses aggressively surmounted motorcycles.

In January 1967, Morse paused from her frantic maneuvers to inventory her latest passions in a characteristically breathless monologue: "I'm working in kinetics and I'm working on my psychedelic collection which I'm taking to the University of Toronto for a psychedelic type of festival—professors, scientists are going—Leary is going—the Fugs are going—I'm making light dresses—I'm making dresses that make noises, I'm making dresses that whisper, dresses that smell."

Not all New York's fashion happenings invoked Dionysus. Some events hailed a new dawn, comparing augeries of the future. Deanna Littell remembers an extravaganza held on a spring night in 1967 at an amphitheater in Central Park. *Glamour* had solicited a number of designer's projections for the anticipated dress of the college student of 2000. "We could do anything we wanted, and we were asked to include a written rationale." Stan Herman, "then as now the most politically aware of the New York designers," sought a solution to racial polarization. He envisioned an invention enabling humans to change their color at will. "You'd have a box in your house," recalled Littell, "you'd go into it in the morning, and press a button. You could be blue or green or whatever color suited your fancy that morning." Herman's model was all blue.

Littell predicted "a chest containing one's entire wardrobe—drip-dry body stockings which could be rolled up and fitted into cubbyholes." Littell's armoire was fitted with a handle and cover and became a convertible valise, so that "your wardrobe could travel with you anywhere." Littell postulated that "life was becoming so mechanized that people would try to keep anything organic close to them in their environment—even if that eventually became a glass

Twiggy with painted vinyl Tiger Morse dress, 1967

bubble." Her model was fashion editor Kezia Keeble, whose body was painted "à la Veruschka with vines and flowers trailing down her limbs." Keeble wore a body stocking and a draped chiffon skirt painted with flowers by Richard Julio, a frequent *Glamour* illustrator. Littell borrowed transparent high-heeled shoes designed by *haute* shoe designer Beth Levine, through which Keeble's tendril-painted feet were visible. "The idea was a portable earth environment."

The greening of Manhattan and its fashion industry seemed undeniable by the final years of the '60s. Alighting in New York from Rome in the spring of 1969, Pilar Crespi—today director of public relations for Krizia, Inc.—found Manhattan's streets "filled with energy, as they are today, but it was a very young energy. People were not so much into the business world; they were more into going through a transition moment in life." The beleaguered middle class was fleeing to the suburbs, inner-city crime and decay were more visible than ever, yet New York in the late '60s was also permeated with the invincible optimism of youth. "New York today is the most swinging town in the world," Halston said in January 1968. "Forget what they say about London. I've found that people here are more inventive—and so is the California hippie movement." New York appeared, in the late '60s, willing to nurture the dreams of young, aspiring achievers in the fine and decorative arts. In 1967, twenty-six-year-old Joan Sibley and twenty-five-year-old Dory Coffee opened a made-to-order business in Sibley's two-bedroom apartment near Sutton Place. Their monthly rent was $150. The firm's workroom-cum-living space was littered with fabric bolts and dress samples. It was crowded with four seamstresses. Their showroom, such as it was, hardly compared to Mainbocher's salon decorated with a cloud-strewn Baroque ceiling fresco. That hardly mattered to the *Women's Wear Daily* "goddesses," Kennedy dynasty matrons, and cynosures of the cinema and pop constellations who patronized their business. By this date, nothing could have been more delectable and *au courant* than its aura of youthful spontaneity. They bought most of their fabrics at Poli's, on 57th Street, a textile house stocking remnants from Seventh Avenue upscale lines. "We'd turn a fabric Seventh Avenue was making into a drop-dead evening look into a blouse you could wear with jeans."

Coming from small towns in Pennsylvania, both women discovered how New York, too, could be subdivided into many tiny networks rippling across the surface of a huge metropolis.

Exotic shoes bagged by Tiger Morse for the opening stock of her Kaleidescope in 1964

Andy Warhol with Vogue *photographer Berry Berenson at a late-night, late-'60s repast in the custom-order salon opened by Halston in 1968 and festooned with African cloth by interior decorator Angelo Donghia*

Andy Warhol and Penelope Tree amid a Factory assemblage in 1968

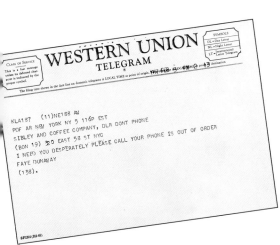

WESTERN UNION
TELEGRAM

KLA187   (11)NE188 AM
POF AR NEW YORK NY 5 116P EST
SIBLEY AND COFFEE COMPANY, DLR DONT PHONE
(BON 19) 30 EAST 58 ST NYC
I NEED YOU DESPERATELY PLEASE CALL YOUR PHONE IS OUT OF ORDER
FAYE DUNAWAY
(138).

*Telegram from Faye Dunaway to Sibley and Coffee.
Sibley today is an antique dealer, Coffee a painter and
goldsmith.*

"Word of mouth made us," Sibley says. While the old-guard couture designed largely for wealthy wives, Sibley and Coffee designed equally for women like themselves who had come to New York to "make it"—women for whom, as Joan Sibley recalled, "marriage could wait." They were walking advertisements for their own work at the celebratory forums New York flocked to in the '60s. "Dory would go out dancing in something we'd made for her and the next day we'd get phone calls."

At Sibley and Coffee, see-through chiffon blouses were safeguarded by strategically placed pockets cut out of two or three layers of fabric. In the patois of the '60s, their clothes were "kicky": more creative and offbeat than those of the rajahs of Seventh Avenue, but not as radical as those of Pop Fashion. "An eighth of an inch can make all the difference in fit and appearance," claimed Joan Sibley. Her business thrived on applying the couture's sense of proportion to the excess-intensive styles of the decade.

THE WEST COAST

When the hippie culture of San Francisco burst into international visibility in 1967, the world's attention focused on a paradoxical aesthetic of opulence and austerity. Though they rejected the trappings of wealth, the trophies of bourgeois status striving, the hippies' clothes often incorporated embroidery as intricate as a *haute couture* ball gown. Instead of a workroom seamstress, however, such embellishment was often the handiwork of the same woman wearing the garment—loomed as a declaration of independence from the anonymity of postindustrial standardization.

In the eyes of the media, San Francisco suddenly replaced London as the new incubator of youthful mores. "The hippie revolution," George Melly claims in *Revolt into Style*, "killed the Swinging London image of the pop dandy and dolly frugging in an 'in' discotheque stone dead." A profound cross-fertilization actually existed between the two youth capitals. Certainly, Mod clothes were the springboard for the hippies' improvisations, while the LSD-influenced iconography of the hippies transformed the landscape of Swinging London. A symbolic marriage was effected when the Beatles joined the cavalcade streaming through Haight-Ashbury. "Lennon especially . . . the hard-man sprouted hair and grannie specs and beamed and beamed."

Throughout 1965 and 1966 a parallel aesthetic was developing in both cities that subverted prior gauges of fashionability. London was cannibalizing and fragmenting ancient couture found at antique stalls; San Francisco was discovering humbler specimens of handwork at the Goodwill thrift shops and becoming engrossed in the lore of the frontier West and the American Indian. Haight-Ashbury's orgiastic and egalitarian utopia asked its participants to sever old loyalties and prior identities. New clothes were essential to this rite of passage. Divesting themselves of the uniforms of the prevailing hierarchies, these dissidents devised masquerades that were incomprehensible to the noninitiated. Their clothes facilitated the dissolution of societal conditioning and the unbridled development of novel life-styles. In its early months, Haight-Ashbury was suffused with the euphoria of what it took to be carte-blanche. "Why not dance any way you feel like, look any way you feel like?" Linda Gravenites, the community's paradigmatic fashion designer, asked herself in unison with hundreds of others.

Like London, San Francisco had long been a haven for mavericks and a cradle of countercultures. When Gravenites arrived there in 1959, she burned with a revolutionary zeal as fervid as that of Isadora Duncan seventy years earlier. She was fleeing a Quaker hamlet on the edge of the Mojave desert outside Los Angeles. Gravenites immersed herself in San Francisco's beatnik community. As the city's social structure again shifted, she found herself a pioneering member of the hippie colony. Gravenites blossomed into a Haight-Ashbury coutu-

Gernreich with models Ellen Harth and Leon Bing in knit dresses with vinyl inserts from his spring 1968 collection for Harmon Knitwear

rier. Her clothes were painstakingly made to the measure of her friends in the hippie nexus. They went to the pages of *Vogue* and articulated the San Francisco look at its most archetypal. Her pastiches of velvet, lace, and second-skin synthetics echoed the hippies' simultaneous embrace of tribal and futuristic modes. "They would turn to the past, but revel in the present," Myra Friedman writes in *Buried Alive*, her biography of Janis Joplin, Gravenites's consummate client. "Neon, day-glo, electricity, chemicals—all would bring the Kingdom of God."

As a teenager, Gravenites dreamed of designing ballet costumes: "They weren't bound to reality—they're quintessential. They can be breathtakingly beautiful and strange and yet they must also be utterly functional. They were the antithesis of the push-'em-up bras and the waist cinches and everything else we were armored with in the '50s." Little could she have dreamed that ten years later a sea of humanity would daily float by her apartment window as outlandishly costumed as any corps de ballet.

Arriving in San Francisco "a totally naive nineteen-year old," Gravenites met and married Patrick Cassady, a logger, welder, and notorious renegade. After their divorce two years later, she married Nick Gravenites, folk singer and, later, rock musician. Having made her own

The West Coast was the new Jerusalem of the 1960s.

(ABOVE) Linda Gravenites design for Janis Joplin in 1967: velvet vest and pants over a chiffon blouse

(RIGHT) Janis Joplin in a Linda Gravenites tunic and pants, cannibalized from a lace tablecloth in 1967

clothes since outfitting childhood dolls, Gravenites began selling embroidered shifts at a shop called The Hatch in Stinson Beach. "Nick went off to Chicago to pursue his music. 'Have a good time!' I told him. 'I'm staying here and doing what I started.'"

Turning out ten shifts a week taught her the durability of chain stitch. "A mass of chain stitch lying flat is almost an eighth of an inch thick and it's *strong*." When a favorite pair of jeans kept ripping, Gravenites experimented with floral embroidery to reenforce the frayed sections of her jeans. She was inspired by a Bay Area folk singer, Jean Ball, for whom she had made a number of garments. Ball had embroidered tiny flowers along the hem of a pair of jeans. "There was great appeal in turning something damaged into something nicer than it had been its pristine form," Gravenites explains. "I'd never seen anything like them before.

My jeans got stared at a whole lot. 'Turn around,' people would urge me as I walked through Golden Gate Park. 'Let me look at those!' Two years later they were on the market."

When the beatniks' North Beach settlement surrendered to commercial appropriation, many of the dispossessed migrated to the blocks radiating from the intersection of Haight and Ashbury streets. The area was then "a San Francisco State College student paradise," Charles Perry notes in his 1984 study *The Haight-Ashbury*. Among its assets it boasted "beautiful, cheap Victorians, a tolerably peaceful population with no one ethnic group predominating, and even its own private strip of the park, the eight-block-long Panhandle."

Gravenites had seen the beat movement decline into "a subculture revolving around speed. People were still hanging out, but they were a different bunch of people. They weren't poets and philosophers. They were drug addicts." Haight-Ashbury's renaissance, too, pivoted on a chemical ingestion, but one that, its champions claimed, was not addicting and could reveal cosmic epiphanies. Was it the contrasting character of the two drugs that determined the temperamental difference in the two dissident communities? The hippie ethos was "an affirmation rather than a disenchanted rejection," Gravenites claims. "It was so much more joyous. People started looking at each other on the street and smiling."

The dress of San Francisco's counterculture harmonized with the psychedelic light shows at the city's rock halls.

The nascent hippie community nailed its sartorial colors to the mast when it turned out en masse for the dance held by the Family Dog commune at Longshoreman's Hall in October 1965. "They came as if there might never be anything like it again," Perry relates. "They were in Mod clothes, Victorian suits, and granny gowns, Old West outfits, pirate costumes, free-form costumes." The Family Dog's celebration marked the ribbon-cutting of the weekly—then nightly—ritual at which the local clans paraded their psychedelic adornment at rock dances in the city's ballrooms.

"At the early dances," Gravenites remembers, "you knew everybody—if not by name, by sight. There'd be maybe two hundred people," she tallies. "When the Jefferson Airplane or

Tie-dying was one of the atavistic crafts investigated by the hippies.

the Grateful Dead weren't onstage playing, they were in the audience carrying on with the rest of us. They were just other friends who happened to be playing the music you danced to.

"People dressed no more bizarrely than they would to walk down Haight Street," she recalls. "We were dressing up to go have a grand time and to be looked at, but mostly to please ourselves. That was what was so exciting. No purpose, no ulterior motive to getting dressed except fun. It's pleasurable to look strange or beautiful or medieval or American Indian."

While Gravenites had experienced the beatnik creed as "a rejection of all worldly values—including beauty," the hippie millennium constructed paeans to the glories of the senses. *Time* contrasted the beat's erstwhile haunt to the hippies' stomping ground: "North Beach was a study in black and white; the Haight-Ashbury is a crazy quilt of living color."

While boutiques eventually proliferated throughout Haight-Ashbury, prefabricated, off-the-peg looks were antithetical to the iconoclasm of the original community. "We got pretty scathing about 'store-bought hip' that didn't come from the soul," Gravenites remembers.

In 1964, Gravenites hated doing custom work: "It took too much time; it was too arduous." But a sea change had occurred; she now sought to crystallize the spirit of anyone for whom she designed. Gravenites was working for San Francisco's Committee Theater, an off-center improvisational group closely allied to the anarchic happenings of the hippies. "It wasn't enough anymore. I decided it was real limiting to clothe a character in a play, because inevitably your clothes are designed to portray one facet primarily," she relates. "The stage clothes zero in on the trait which will suit the mechanisms of the plot. It's rarely a complete person—the costumes underscore that salient aspect. "Why not take this a step or two further, I thought, and match a whole person? We're all born with different and unique talents, and that was mine—the rest was craft."

"Mimi Fariña gave me the nicest verbal valentine once. I'd just brought her a blouse of ecru-colored silk crêpe-backed satin, embroidered with antique red glass beads. She put it on, looked in the mirror, and said 'Oh, Linda, it's me as I've always dreamed of being!'"

In 1968, Janis Joplin told *Vogue* that Gravenites "turns them out slowly and turns them out well and only turns them out for those she likes." In a 1986 interview, Tina Turner recalled that it was the clothes Gravenites made for Joplin that sparked Turner's own pursuit of riotous finery. They first met during the summer of 1967. Having just tasted international acclaim at the Monterey Pop Festival the previous June, Joplin now asked Gravenites to make her an outfit for an upcoming appearance. The two women developed an instant rapport and became roommates in an apartment on Lyon Street as the Summer of Love slowly ebbed. Hints of autumn peeked over the horizon, but the City was still bathed in warm sunshine. To the north and south, the Panhandle and Buena Vista Park nestled below the tiny balcony on which she put the finishing hand touches to a lace pantsuit for Joplin. Sailing out of their living room hi-fi, Aretha Franklin sang the praises of "Groovin." Not immune to the strife that had begun to fracture the Haight, Gravenites nonetheless basked in the ripe smell of a San Francisco Indian summer and in the realization that philosophical evolution and vocational focus had merged.

Today, in a studio deep in the Redwoods, one hundred miles north of the city, Gravenites creates stained-glass windows on commission. She has kept few mementoes of her former life. From her attic she retrieves a box marked "SILK ." Among the remnants it contains is a magnificent chiffon figured with velvet, the last of a yardage out of which she cut a blouse for Joplin. Gravenites dispersed most of her supplies when she phased herself out of the music world. "I was tired of watching my friends kill themselves."

"As a child, my mother taught me how to use the same Singer featherweight model sewing machine which I own today. There *are* some attachments you can append, but I never had any patience with attachments, so if I couldn't do it on that I did it by hand. If I'd been concerned about making a good living from my clothes, I wouldn't, I *couldn't* have done things the way I was doing them in the '60s. I was unreasonable. I wanted every stitch, every buttonhole to be tiny and delicate and perfect. 'Good God, Linda!' even Janis would say."

Two faces of Los Angeles: Folk-rock chanteuse Linda Ronstadt, then a member of the Stone Ponys, wears a Betsey Johnson dress sold at the Beverly Hills Paraphernalia. Faye Dunaway at the premiere of the film Camelot *in 1967—Dunaway was one of the few stars of the "New Hollywood," who dressed according to the lavish requisites of old.*

It didn't seem odd that Seventh Avenue's most influential designer lived and worked in Los Angeles. Rudi Gernreich's detachment from the shibboleths of the fashion world was reinforced by his geographic isolation. When most of Seventh Avenue's upper echelon courted high-society clients with warmed-over couture, Gernreich maintained a low-profile personal life and produced pared-down clothes targeted for the new life-styles into which women were venturing. Gernreich's clothes reflected his orientation toward Bauhaus functionalism and his early involvement in dance. They materialized in unusual fabrics and dissonant color harmonies and were shot through with a streak of bizarrerie. "His clothes hang like paper in the cupboard," British *Vogue* noted in 1964, "but take on a terrific and dramatic shape on the body." To New Yorkers, his clothes beckoned with the sensual vigor of health-conscious Southern California and its prevailing casualness: "A grand dress is totally boring," Gernreich said in 1967.

Twice a year Gernreich left his aerie in the Hollywood Hills and traveled to his Seventh Avenue showroom to unveil two companion collections: a knitwear group for Harmon Knitwear

Dennis Hopper and Brooke Hayward were among the first in Los Angeles to amass an extensive collection of American Pop Art. At their West Hollywood home in 1964 (clockwise): model Lydia Fields, art dealer Irving Blum, TV producer Bert Berman, Peggy Moffitt, Hopper, painter Billy Al Bengston (on floor), and Brooke Hayward's son. Fields and Moffitt wear Gernreich's chiffon cocktail dresses with self-fabric veils in Klimt-like prints of red/pink and green/pink.

and an upmarket line he manufactured himself. "His approach from Los Angeles invariably foretells a period of unrest and upheaval in the fashion world," reported Lewis H. Lapham of the *Saturday Evening Post*. "The sophisticated ladies who rule that world . . . wait eagerly for his newest outrage. Mindful of his reputation as the most extreme, the farthest-out of all American dress designers, Rudi seldom disappoints them."

Throughout the '60s, Gernreich was alternately vilified and lionized. The media loved the instant news provided by his often heretical offerings: suit jackets with one notched and one rounded lapel, satin tuxedos, and most notoriously, a topless bathing suit. Fellow designers frequently carped; Norman Norell returned his Coty when Gernreich received one for the collection in which his clashing lapel jacket debuted. "Anyone enterprising enough to mass produce a dartboard with Rudi Gernreich's face on it could probably make a small fortune on Seventh Avenue," the *Village Voice* estimated in 1968.

Born into an intellectual Viennese family, Gernreich was introduced to fashion via his aunt's dressmaking salon. The frothy concoctions she turned out provided "an invaluable background," he later recalled. "It taught me what not to do." As a child he planned on becoming a painter, before fleeing the Nazis with his mother in the late '30s and resettling in Los Angeles. A chance encounter with a performance by the Martha Graham troupe changed his life. Gernreich subsequently studied dance and performed for several years with Lester Horton's modern dance troupe. In addition to performing, he designed costumes for the Horton troupe before deciding to pursue a career in fashion design. He moved to New York and apprenticed briefly with a Seventh Avenue manufacturing firm; his stint there was a "disaster," he later recalled. He returned to L.A. in 1951, designed textiles and advertisements, and worked in the costume department at M-G-M. In 1952, he joined forces with Viennese expatriot manufacturer Walter Bass. Their clothes were prominently featured at Jax, the Beverly Hills retail outlet that helped popularize the boutique idea in Los Angeles. During the '50s, Gernreich's clothes for Jax achieved a special cachet among the Hollywood community. "If a studio brought somebody out from the East Coast to make a starlet out of them—I'm talking about the intelligent girls from the Actor's Studio—chances are she'd come in just a plain blouse and pants," explains L.A. designer Bob Rogers. "It was practically required that they go to Jax and get themselves some clothes. They were given several thousand dollars, and Jax would lock his door to the public, and completely outfit that actress. That was almost routine in the '50s. They'd go back to the studios happy—they wouldn't consider Jax clothes a sellout—and the studio would start building an image around that."

Gernreich first earned attention from the fashion world at large for his bathing suits, which eliminated the boning and underpinning customary at the time. His bathing wear earned a special Coty award in 1959. Here, Peggy Moffitt models Gernreich's black wool knit bathing suit, with patent leather belt, for Harmon Knitwear in 1967.

In 1966, Peggy Moffitt posed for London's Queen magazine in Gernreich's white lingerie satin top and lingerie satin pants in a black-and-white print designed by Tzaims Luksus. The broken mirror pin is by Gernreich, and hair styled by Vidal Sassoon.

By the time the '60s were under way, Gernreich had dissolved his association with Bass and opened his own firm. To Peggy Moffitt, Gernreich's favorite model and Muse, he spoke admiringly during the '60s of the work of Courrèges and Paco Rabanne, yet for design inspiration he turned instead, she notes, "to life, to the news of the world." If Le Corbusier had envisioned the house as a machine for living, Gernreich conceived of clothes as unencumbered vessels for vigorous and varied activity. Gernreich was suffused with the versatility of the Bauhaus founding fathers, who had melded high and applied art. Gernreich designed furniture and product containers as well as clothes. In the Bauhaus spirit, he approached fashion as one constituent element in a total design philosophy. For Moffitt, the mentality gulf between Gernreich and other Seventh Avenue wholesale designers was so yawning that "it's almost as though they were in different professions. What he was doing just happened to involve clothing. The be-all and end-all for all those people was clothing—and is today."

Within fashion, Gernreich's principal debt was to the fluid jerseys of Claire McCardell, who, in the 1930s, began producing multi-purpose clothing that was subject to the wearer's manipulation. Her clothes were transformed by wraps, ties, and the wearer's ingenuity. The flexibility afforded by McCardell's clothes was ideal for the automobile-oriented suburban explosion of the postwar years, during which her popularity zoomed, cut off by her untimely death in 1958. Gernreich assumed McCardell's mantle after having spent most of his life witnessing Los Angeles's unbridled expansion. He, too, saw signposts pointing to the age of ever-increasing leisure and convenience that many in the '60s believed technology could provide. "As fashion grows definitely freer and less inhibited," *Time* reported in 1967, "[Gernreich hopes] that all costumes will become inexpensive enough to be worn briefly, then thrown away on a whim."

In 1964, Gernreich's most sensational gesture turned him into a media celebrity overnight. After speculating that, within four or five years, women would regularly go sunbathing topless, he was besieged by so many orders for such a swimsuit that he decided to produce a prototype. Condemned by the Pope, the topless elicited a torrent of correspondence ranging from threats to marriage proposals. Three thousand suits were sold at $25 each. Women picketed, bearing placards reading: "AS MOTHERS WE PROTEST TOPLESS SWIM SUITS." Gernreich responded to the hue and cry by predicting that "The topless, by overstating and exaggerating a new freedom of the body, will make the moderate, *right* amount of freedom acceptable." Gernreich's prophecies were couched both in the seductive tone of whisper and the thundering timbre of declamation. That same year, Gernreich made transparent blouses of lacquered chiffon to be worn under black ciré suits influenced by motorcycle garb—one of many adoptions

Black ciré trouser suit over a lacquered chiffon blouse from Gernreich's fall 1964 collection

from the uniforms of youth culture. "What he sees young people wearing as he drives around Los Angeles in his white Jaguar 3.8 sedan or strolls Manhattan streets is a major source of inspiration," *Time* noted in 1967. "The young are very inventive about what they want to wear," Gernreich said, "how they wear it, and what they want to say with it. I get a great many of my ideas from watching them."

In 1965, Gernreich told Gloria Steinem in the *New York Times Magazine* that during his stint with the Horton dance troupe: "I became less interested in the static details, the decorations of clothes, and more concerned with how they looked in motion. Before, I only considered the body from the neck to the knees, the part that was clothed. Dancing made me aware of what clothes did to the rest of the body; to the hands and feet and head." His clothes silhouetted the movement of the body as truly as the filmy tulle of Giselle's cloudlike skirt or the pliant jersey shroud of a Graham heroine. Gernreich, too, advocated the ease of interchangeable layering, essential to a dancer's practice wear. "Rudi Gernreich opened his show yesterday and said he believed in co-ordination," *WWD* reported in June 1966. "He wasn't kidding—his total look not only comes from head to toe, but from the inside out." Gernreich showed underwear in fabrics coordinated with his sportswear, blurring distinctions between inner and outerware, between the private and public.

In 1967, Gernreich shared a retrospective fashion show at the Fashion Institute of Technology in Manhattan with fellow maverick Elizabeth Hawes, fashion designer, author, and polit-

Dean Martin's daughter, Claudia, in paper dresses from Judith Brewer's Los Angeles boutique

ical activist. In the '30s, while running a Manhattan custom salon, Hawes had published a best-selling treatise, *Fashion Is Spinach*. It was a barbed attack on the unquestioned assumptions according to which most people dressed. Gernreich and Hawes "envisioned clothes as something to be thought about, thought through. Both believed in design and beauty and hated status dressing," Bettina Berch notes in *Radical by Design*, her recent biography of Hawes. Hawes was enjoying a belated recognition after years of exile from the fashion establishment, which had not been enchanted with her broadsides against the American Way throughout the '50s. Gernreich was then at the height of his renown; later that year he would appear on the cover of *Time*. Yet the following year Gernreich withdrew temporarily from the fashion fray. Announcing his sabbatical, he explained: "Anything that is overdesigned or bears too much the stamp of the individual designer is not right." The violent self-expresson of the late '60s seemed to be rendering the fashion designer obsolete. "The moment you design something, it is imposed on people."

They all came to Holly Harp's vestpocket boutique on Sunset Strip—all the chic hippies of Los Angeles. The young stars of popular music and the New Hollywood ferreted out Harp's nostalgic crêpe and exotic batik, her tie-dyed marabou boas, her one-of-a-kind gowns of hand-painted chiffon or matte jersey. As dazzling as her creations looked on the sleek fireflies of upscale L.A., Harp reserved a special sympathy for the grittier glamour of the rock queens who passed through Los Angeles on performing or recording sojourns. They "knew exactly how they wanted to look, but they were so needy—like any woman shopping: 'What do you think? . . . Are my legs O.K.?'" Harp's rapport with these women on the edge stemmed from her firsthand experience of an earlier renegade. "My mother was a fall-down drunk who died when I was nine," Harp recalls. "But she wasn't just a drunk—she was a tremendous rebel. She grew up dancing the Charleston and drinking bathtub gin all night long. I always sensed that my mother wasn't content being a lady. So I had a real love for people who really, really bust out, like Janis or Grace—women who don't keep their pinkie in the air. I only wish they hadn't had to kill themselves in the process."

The modalities of sartorial rebellion in Los Angeles and San Francisco reflected the traditional rivalry between the two cities. To the residents of Haight-Ashbury, "Los Angeles was where you went to shop at stores that *sold clothes*," Linda Gravenites explains. "Here you went to the Goodwill, or made it yourself, or had a friend who did." L.A.'s style-conscious population adopted the northern city's sartorial license wholeheartedly—glossing it, of course, with a flossier veneer than the pocketbooks and ideology of San Francisco encouraged. On

New Year's Eve 1967, "Mama" Michelle Phillips welcomed nine hundred guests to her Bel-Air estate. Fanning across her lawns were "ribbons of wonderful people of all ages" dressed in "feathers and silks, Indian paisleys, beads, saris, Nehru suits, very long hair, sequins, lots of marcasite earrings, aquamarines, all the semiprecious stones that were so popular with young hippies."

Only a few years before becoming, in the words of the *Los Angeles Times*, the city's "doyenne of feathers and fringe," Holly Harp had been a Radcliffe dropout from Upstate New York, "bumming around Acapulco looking for a husband." In 1963 Harp experienced "one of those clear Gestalt realizations: I wanted to make clothes. I wasn't going to look for a rich guy. I was going to go back to school, and have a career, and make money myself." After graduating from North Texas State University with a degree in art and costume design, Harp arrived in Los Angeles with her husband, a doctoral candidate at the University of Southern California. "I really did not know this city or the scene or anything. There used to be a place called The Pleasure Dome on Fairfax. I stumbled in there and I thought I'd arrived in heaven. That was the most happening store in L.A. at the time. It was hard-core rich hippie. I really borrowed my trip from them."

"I started working for a firm downtown that was still doing '50s sheath dresses with zippers. By the late '60s they'd realized something else was happening. They hired me 'cause I looked the part, but I couldn't really cut it. It was a very frenetic scene." At the night school where Harp studied pattern making, a teacher noted her frustration and advised her to strike out on her own. "Buy a little cotton, and sew the dresses up in the back yourself. You could get twenty-five dollars for them."

Harp set up shop on the eastern spur of Sunset Boulevard, the raucous stretch known as the Strip, parade ground for the city's teen and dissident cultures. In former years, Sunset Boulevard hosted Schwabb's Drugstore, and Ciro's and Mogambo's nightclubs—milestones of the old Hollywood. In the '60s, these same premises resounded with the heresies of Lenny Bruce and a galaxy of rock and pop acts. The Strip was conveniently close to the wooded pockets of Laurel Canyon, which, soaring into the Hollywood Hills, was studded with the homes of many rock and pop musicians.

Harp tapped into the street life outside her doorway. "I started with one little jersey dress and began observing people; I really just stood there and learned what to do. I never went into Beverly Hills. I didn't know anything about the larger fashion scene. I considered myself counterculture," she says. Harp became infatuated with the hippies' recycling of cast-offs. "I was

A pregnant Michelle Phillips in 1967, wearing an embroidered robe designed by Toni Scarles of Profils du Monde in Beverly Hills

a junk-store-aholic. I couldn't drive by one without a snake charmer coming up and grabbing me. I would just buy every hand-me-down that they had."

"A lot of people would come in and just reel with horror. An editor from *Women's Wear Daily*, dressed in a severe suit, came to see me. She didn't get it at all." An acidulous Broadway comedienne once arrived when Harp had just finished her first resuscitated drapery. "I was so proud. I actually made it out of a curtain, I told her. She gave me a withering glance: 'It's *obvious*.' I was crushed." Harp recalls, too, a visit by a reigning divinity of the best-dressed census. "She looked around at everything. 'It's not my dish of tea,' she finally said. It was as though a foul odor had hit her."

THE BEAUTIFUL PEOPLE

The traditional cycles of fashion were reversed during the '60s. Adoption by the old guard status corps now could kill rather than bestow the cachet of a style. True believers in the couture gospel, the rich watched in disbelief as young, multiracial apostates replaced the mature, moneyed Caucasian women who had formerly steered fashion's course. To the conservative rich, fashion had been overrun by untouchables. Speaking from her Long Island estate, Mainbocher devotee Mrs. Winston Guest asked in 1967: "Do you think those young girls are ever going to pull themselves together? They should. I'm so tired of them looking like shaggy dogs. Even Boo [her mastiff] has his hair done."

Many in the mainstream of the industry itself continued to believe that the pitchpipes of fashion remained a tiny cabal of women married to modern-day plutocrats. These matrons ranged in age from the forties to the sixties, and they had been raised to make advantageous marriages; the wealth of their husband was the yardstick of their achievement. Some of these women came from prosaic, even squalid backgrounds, some from patrician dynasties. By day, their understated dress and gracious veneers clearly marked their aspired-to distance from the proverbial crassness of the nouveaux riches. By night, however, ostentation bloomed, as hairdos exploded, buttressed with hairpieces into towering concoctions à la Marie Antoinette. Paste jewelry glittered from satin "embassy gowns," while the real McCoy might dazzle at neckline, earlobe, wrist, and bosom. This was the uniform of the Beautiful People, the hyper-consuming exquisites titled by *Vogue* editor-in-chief Diana Vreeland.

Although their wardrobes were usually financed by their husbands, the fashion statements of these women were often their sole bids for a distinction apart from their spouses. During the '60s they saw their authority buffeted, as the young, who possessed a commodity that could not be bought, became the power brokers. Mrs. Loel Guinness, who had been crowned "fashion's first lady" by *WWD* in 1963, lamented in 1968: "Ten years ago women dressed well and looked dignified. Today if you dress like a decent person, you are made to feel you are a million years old. If you dress young, you look like an idiot. What choice is there?"

Jacqueline Kennedy was sui generis among this echelon. She was younger than most of her colleagues in the best-dressed pantheon; indeed, her husband's administration had presaged the youthful tenor of the '60s. Until her marriage to Aristotle Onassis in 1968, she was probably the most influential fashion figure for the American masses. Insufficiently adventurous and too casual (after her return to private life) for many of the fashion pundits, her touch was nonetheless charmed. At a Manhattan lunch in December 1966, she wore a skirt that rose several inches above her knee, thereby ratifying the miniskirt for American women over

Evening dresses from Sophie Gimbel's custom salon at Saks Fifth Avenue

Vicomtesse Jacqueline de Ribes and Marquis Raymondo de Larrain at a masquerade ball

thirty. Like many affluent women in the '60s, Mrs. Onassis hedged her bets by offering a strangely ambivalent reading of fashion's lexicon. She shortened her skirts, but retained the genteel accoutrements of yore, sometimes accessorizing her minidresses with the formal long gloves she had worn as first lady.

Marking the zenith—or nadir—of the best-dressed *mondaines* was the duchess of Windsor, whose obsessive preoccupation with personal grooming was legendary. The duchess's moves during this decade offered an indictment of society's conditioning and the vagaries of

Jacqueline Kennedy in 1965

personal vanity. The seventy-year-old who had dreamed, as a girl, of becoming a doctor or an explorer now occupied herself with a futile attempt, via plastic surgery and relentless fashion consumption, to muffle the tolling of the clock. The fashion media breathlessly inventoried the fifty-eight trunks carried off her ocean liner when it dropped anchor in New York; each of her *mots* on fashion and the fashionable was faithfully reported.

With London a hotbed of sedition and Paris under siege, many socialites turned to the Roman couture. In Rome, couturier Frederico Forquet cooed sympathetically: "The 1960s are the most inelegant moment of our century. We live in a carnival atmosphere with no specific tendencies. There are too many contrasts and too much confusion in fashion. There's no single spirit."

"Women are still a luxury in Italy," Princess Luciana Pignatelli told Brigid Keenan of Britain's *Nova* magazine. Surveying the Roman landscape, Keenan concurred. "We've almost forgotten what full time playboys and girls are; in Rome they still exist." Valentino Garavani was perhaps the most internationally renowned Roman couturier; his clothes crystallized the languor pervading couture in the city of la dolce vita. Eugenia Sheppard noted the "extravagant, untroubled mood of female luxury that Valentino has brought back to fashion." The friendship of the Beautiful People was instrumental to his success; in 1967, at a party Valentino threw to celebrate an award bestowed by Neiman-Marcus, the couturier duly printed a roll call of his rich and titled customers.

Brown moiré dress created by Princess Irene Galitzene of Rome in 1967

The upheavals of the '60s offered liberation rather than oblivion to some of the decade's social pillars. Gloria Vanderbilt displayed a signal metamorphosis toward the end of the decade. In February 1967, the forty-three-year-old had denounced contemporary fashions as "grotesque. . . . Fashion seems like such a hodge-podge now." By October of that year, however, *WWD* declared that Vanderbilt was "a new woman. She's moving with the times." "You go out on the street and you feel this marvelous spirit of change," Vanderbilt exclaimed. "It's a terrific time for women. They have more freedom. . . . Women have a choice of what they want to do and be."

"I'm spending much less money this fall and having much more fun with fashion" Vanderbilt exclaimed, as she began circulating in the fantasy realm of late '60s fashions. Vanderbilt preferred custom-made creations from Adolpho, the society milliner who began designing clothes in mid decade. For the Manhattan opening of a show of Vanderbilt's artwork in May 1968, she wore what Adolpho described as "an Elizabethan dress," inspired by Vanderbilt's *Queen Elizabeth with Bows* collage. Crowned by an enormous ruff of layers of organdy and silver lace, Vanderbilt's dress was contoured with lilac and pink ruching on a tight Mannerist bodice, over a full skirt of silver lace over lavender organza.

Marriage was the Rubicon for most of the dowagers of fashion; these women were always known by the husband's first and second names. Their impeccable grooming both advertised and legitimized their husband's fortune, for in fashion, as in fairy tales, beauty and goodness are synonymous. Flaunting their husband's largess followed the classic pattern recorded by Thorstein Veblen in his turn-of-the-century exegesis *Theory of the Leisure Class*. Yet the prod-

Lace-edged crêpe-de-chine blouse and mink-hemmed velvet skirt, designed in 1967 by Chester Weinberg, one of Seventh Avenue's bright young men of the '60s; muff by Jacques Kaplan; satin-tipped brown velvet boots by Julianelli

igal display of the trinkets a man had given her acquired uncomfortable associations as women began demanding economic enfranchisement. "Too much jewelry makes you look . . . as if you were rejected by lots of rich, old men, who paid you off," Mary Quant noted in 1967. Reporting on the September 1967 opening of the Metropolitan Opera season, Eugenia Sheppard identified a new trend at galas: "the rise of the career woman as a fashion figure. This year the pros, the hard workers, look incomparably better than most of the wealthy women who would settle for jewel-embroidered dresses, obviously expensive, and let it go at that."

On a January night in 1965, Anne McDonnell Ford appeared at El Morocco in a Courrèges shiny white top and black skirt and white boots. Her namesake daughter accompanied her, dressed in a conservative black dress and matching pumps. "Which one is the mother?" WWD's Carol Bjorkman wondered, expressing a confusion that would reverberate through the decade. Women who adopted the costumes of youth were accused of betraying their dignity, of abdicating the obligations of middle age. Age, as much as rank and occasion, regulated the appearance of women who subscribed to canons of appropriateness. "Until the '60s," Kennedy Fraser writes in *The Fashionable Mind*, "it was still entirely thinkable that a woman's style of dress should define both her age and her marital status, just as it did in the nineteenth century." An enduring legacy of the '60s is the abolition of many categories of age-specific clothing. The youth craze of the '60s precipitated the fitness mania of the following decade; today's thirty-five- or forty-five-year-old woman appears much younger than her counterpart of twenty years ago.

Conventional wisdom concerning the '60s holds that the decade's fashions comprised a conspiracy by designers to transform women back into little girls. In fact, Seventh Avenue, as much as the Paris couture, resisted acknowledging the revolutionary fashions created for and by youth. In 1967, Marilyn Bender extolled Jacques Tiffeau's showings as "one of the few presentations on Seventh Avenue that is relevant to the contemporary spirit blowing through London and the ready-to-wear fashion market of Paris." Established designers were loath to recognize a movement that challenged the assumptions by which their clientele dressed. In addition, most, if not all, high-volume manufacturers nodded to fashion's revolutionary cast only by chopping inches off the prim suits and bouffant ballgowns they doggedly produced. The '60s seemed like a millenium; it was but a handful of years, but the latitude it introduced would take a long time to reach vast segments of women. During the '60s, many women "went on wearing conventional garments whether suited to them or not," William O'Neil writes in *Coming Apart.* "It was the rare elderly woman who looked good in deep-necked, bare-armed evening dresses, yet few took advantage of the formal pants suits and party pajamas that enabled older people to be in style without exposing the ravages of time."

The generation of mainstream Seventh Avenue designers who arose in the wake of Norell and his colleagues made clothes that appealed to a wide cross-section of upscale women. Neither Seventh Avenue's customers nor its designers challenged traditional ideas of femininity and clothing design. They elucidated no visionary rationales. *WWD* reported in 1967 that the typical customer of Seventh Avenue's Donald Brooks "knows about Haights-Ashbury [sic] and Anti-Establishment London. But she disassociates." Brooks himself postulated: "Until she takes her first trip to the moon she will not begin to dress for it. In the meantime she will go on enjoying her Impressionist paintings and the 18th century furniture."

Seventh Avenue's achievement during the '60s was a triumph of social mobility. The expanding media coverage given fashion made American designers celebrities, as the Parisian couturiers had been since the days of Poiret's prominence. Seventh Avenue's young lions, formerly shunned because of the Italian and Jewish background of the industry, became sought-after men-about-town for the women they dressed.

Having often climbed from ignominious economic origins, the couture courtiers of the

Beautiful People reacted defensively when the privelege to which they had aspired was challenged. "Those hippies in their rags are only something to laugh at," Valentino sneered in 1967. "I believe only in high fashion." "I'm not concerned with the hippies, the Village look or the London look," said James Galanos, who made severe clothes in unusual fabrications. "It's ridiculous to say they're making fashion. Most of them wouldn't be allowed in the best restaurants in town." Galanos bristled at the rage for antique clothing. "Heaven forbid," he shuddered, "a woman in her '40s or '50s—even '20s or '30s—going out and buying a smelly old thing that someone else has worn."

For the venturesome among the rich, the '60s provided a unique opportunity to slum among bohemia's picturesque inhabitants. Their defiance of conventional dress and behavior piqued a titillated curiosity. The '60s were characterized by a new cultural miscegenation, in which bare feet might comingle with black ties, as happened at the benefit opening night for the New York's Electric Circus discotheque in June 1967.

The trappings of Haight-Ashbury were *de rigeur* throughout the summer of 1967. At a party thrown in Los Angeles, interior decorator Tony Duquette wore Indian beads and a beaded vest to greet honored guest Dame Margot Fonteyn. The ballerina's brown and white Saint Laurent dress was accessorized with a necklace of Indian beads and a bracelet of tiny bead flowers. "They threw them upon the stage after our last performance in San Francisco," she explained. At the party, two long-haired young men operated a psychedelic sound and lighting system. Six months later, Halston commented on a party thrown in New York by heiress Cathy McAuley in the triplex apartment she had inherited from her grandmother. "It was what is happening—young . . . staid . . . hippies . . . all mixed together. Nobody knew anyone, but that didn't matter. Before it did."

As the tree was bent, so were some twigs inclined. Amanda Mortimer, the daughter of eternally best-dressed Mrs. William Paley, toed the line gracefully. Elevated into prominence when she married Carter Burden, Mrs. Burden accentuated her frail beauty by dressing like a Dresden Alice. Other leaders among the *jeunesse dorée* staked out more exotic frontiers. Mary "Minnie" Cushing, a sloe-eyed Newport debutante, began working for Oscar de la Renta, reporting by motorbike to his midtown showroom. Cushing burst into full peahen refulgence following her marriage to photographer Peter Beard, when she began handcrafting leather belts that were retailed at New York boutiques. Cushing's long, heavy, dark hair and willowy figure were gorgeously showcased in the low-slung pants and leather vests of the late '60s.

"I wanted to live away from the family and I wanted to work," Pilar Crespi recalls, "to live a kind of life that I couldn't do in Italy." Crespi, today director of public relations for Krizia, Inc., was the daughter of publicist Count Rudolpho Crespi and his wife, former model Consuelo Crespi, *Vogue*'s Rome liaison. Dressed in Valentino's re-embroidered lace and three hairpieces, Crespi had attended the storybook ball thrown by Portugal's Patino dynasty; in New York, however, she lived in T-shirts and pants. "I wasn't interested in doing the conservative club life in New York. So that's why I went to the Village. We've never had anything like it in Rome, and probably never will." Downtown she was enraptured by "the whole movement of the flower power and the flower children. I had never seen anything like that. To me, coming from Europe, it was amazing."

To Jane Holzer, the louche half-world of Andy Warhol and his disciples offered a delicious contrast to the sterility of Park Avenue's haute bourgeoisie. The wife of a real-estate princeling, Holzer was the first "Superstar" incarnated by Andy Warhol, who christened her "Baby Jane" in 1964. "My husband doesn't mind my being in underground movies," she explained. "It's

(Left) Pilar Crespi in Rome, late '60s

(Below) Jane Holzer in 1967

Pop Art patroness Ethel Scull (seen here with Thomas Hoving) and her husband, Robert, epitomized the swinging new rich of the '60s. The organza skirt and blouse are by Adolpho, 1968.

better than sitting around all day having lunches." Holzer sported one of the largest heads of back-combed hair on record, championed the Rolling Stones on their first American tour, and dressed in of-the-moment couture as well as ready-to-wear.

"What's happened to the great ladies of fashion?" *WWD* asked in 1968. "They've stopped experimenting at a time when everybody else is. They've become dull and secure." Watching the fossilized attire of erstwhile deities, the newspaper commented, "You'd never know this was the year of doing your own thing in fashion." The Beautiful People were temporarily buried in the shower of individuality that exploded at the end of the '60s. The sartorial indulgence of the rich was frowned upon in the egalitarian climate of the day. As some pockets of the wealthy began espousing liberal causes and dabbling in "Radical Chic," overt profligacy became wholly infra dig. In 1969, pop art patroness Ethel Scull confessed: "Prices are so expensive that you feel guilty spending that kind of money, especially with what's happening in the world today." As the '60s ended, many believed that the time-honored rituals of ostentation and display were extinct. "Money no longer has value as a status symbol," Rudi Gernreich theorized. "It's tacky to flaunt it, and modern, thinking people are not putting it on their backs."

MEN

"Why should the male not also be a sexual object?" Rudi Gernreich asked in 1969, throwing the gauntlet in the the face of received values. Unlike the century's earlier fashion upheavals, those of the '60s affected men's as well as women's clothing; indeed, the most accurate barometer of fashion's aberrational climate during the decade may be the reformation it brought in men's attitudes. Personal adornment had long been the paramount province of women's self-expression. For almost 150 years, man's empowerment had been predicated in part on his disdain for the female realm of vanity and titivation. While women had appropriated staples of men's wardrobes many times during these decades, rarely, if *ever*, had the reverse been true; to explore women's domain would have undermined man's superiority. "For years, men have been in uniform while women were imprisoned in fashion. Now they are free to dress in terms of how they feel about themselves," Marshall McLuhan discoursed in 1968.

Whereas changes in men's wear had traditionally been confined to fractional modifications in lapel or sleeve, vistas in men's dress now appeared that had not been seen since the days of the rococo. Men sprouted resplendent plumage in sumptuous colors and fabrics. Contemporary observers saw "the peacock revolution" as an outgrowth of women's lobby for economic parity. In 1967, Marilyn Bender observed women "rethinking their place in society. . . . The respective roles of men and women . . . [are] . . . being revised." Should women achieve economic independence, commentators speculated, their mate's financial wherewithal would no longer be his ace card in the game of seduction. In 1964, James Laver had offered this analysis: "Women can now afford to choose as husbands men who attract them as men, not providers." Laver predicted that men would now "begin to dress for physical attraction. The erotic could then transfer back to man's dress."

Underlying all was the new premise that the essence of masculinity or femininity was not bestowed by clothing but was instead immanent in the individual. Gender identities were posited as more complex and ambiguous than had previously been allowed—points on a continuum rather than opposite poles. The new repertory of emotional and active stances for women and men were echoed in fashion. One outgrowth was unisex, which presupposed totally interchangeable attire for both sexes. Gernreich interpreted "unisex as a total statement about the equality of men and women. . . . The male is emerging from aesthetic exile as women achieve their freedom."

Straws in the wind auguring the '60s blowout in menswear appeared early in the preceding decade. In 1950, a group of tailors in London's exclusive Savile Row, the bastion of aristocratic men's clothiers, introduced a silhouette recalling the halcyon days of the British empire. The

Men and women in sheepskin

components of their neo-Edwardian look were narrow trousers, ornate waistcoats, and long jackets with narrow lapels. These suits were intended for smart young gentlemen-about-town wishing to rebuke the austerity regime of the Socialist government. While Mayfair's young peers did not rise to the bait, the vestigial finery of the new styles became red flags of rebellion for working-class outlaws in the proletariat districts of South London—the "Teddy Boys."

By the early '60s, the Teddy Boy *Weltenschaung* had fizzled, and media attention was commanded by the Mods and the Rockers, adversarial fraternities with pronounced sartorial profiles. Mods were working-class bucks who co-opted the fastidiousness of the Savile Row customer. Rockers romanced their motorcycles and accoutered themselves in burly leather

Unisex luminiscence worn and designed by Diana Dew

Designer Giorgio Sant' Angelo

141

John Stephens in one of his Carnaby Street boutiques

jackets, jeans, and heavy boots. The first generation of Mods was made up of zealots who sought out local custom tailors to realize their special designs. The Mods who followed, however, evinced as much interest in rock 'n' roll and in their female companions, the "dollies," as they did in clothes. It was to this wave that the ready-to-wear men's stores of Carnaby Street were directed.

A byway hidden behind the main shopping thoroughfares of Oxford and Regent streets, Carnaby Street became a fashion center largely because of retailer John Stephen, who shrewdly exploited the street's former position as a corridor of men's mail-order swimwear concerns. Their catalogues were targeted at homosexuals, who, traditionally disenfranchised, were exempt from centrist sartorial dogma and provided a ready audience for experimentation in menswear. By 1966, John Stephen owned nine men's boutiques on Carnaby Street, known now as "Peacock Alley," and its homosexual associations had evaporated. Women's boutiques proliferated, too, and they also established men as objects of sexual and decorative speculation: topless male shop assistants waited on customers at the women's store Sweet Fanny Adams.

"Mods are ahead of everyone in fashion," *WWD* registered in 1964. "By the time their look catches on, they're on to something else." The working class was usurping the customs of the fashion-conscious wealthy by abandoning a style once it was disseminated to the mainstream. But the Mods lost caste following a series of violent confrontations with the Rockers

Man's caftan from Michael Rainey at Hung on You, and a woman's dress by Ossie Clark of Quorum in 1967

in 1964. Fashion looked for new, more poetic role models, finding them in nineteenth-century dandies and bohemians, who defied the standardization of industrial society by forging alternative life-styles and dress.

The vanguard of menswear became the unique boutiques that opened across London. At Michael Rainey's shop Hung on You, in King's Road, "Smartie Suits" passed into the British vernacular. Named after the pastel-colored candies, they were well-cut suits in pale striped pink, blue, and yellow sharkskin. Out of old kilim rugs, Michael Rainey made men's boots; some of his wares, such as a gold lamé evening shirt, were unisex. At Granny Takes a Trip, another nodal point on King's Road, clothes were gender-specific, yet "everything was androgynous by nature," recalls Nigel Waymouth, one of the store's founders. Granny's was designed as a stopping place where men and women could "come in as a couple and come out 'kitted out' in the new clothes."

Two years after graduating from the University of London with an economics degree, Waymouth went into partnership with twenty-one-year-old Sheila Troy, and John Pearse, nineteen, who had been trained as a tailor in Savile Row. Granny Takes a Trip was named in deference to the resurgence of antique clothes and the wonders of the LSD experience. It opened in March 1966, selling secondhand clothes as well as a few shirts its charter team had designed. "We can offer an exclusive thing to everyone," they promised soon after the store opened, "because we rarely find two dresses which are identical. You can't repeat what we sell and the prices are reasonable."

Waymouth and his colleagues soon concentrated on original designs with a period flavor. They eagerly "hunted around places anywhere, finding materials that were interesting. We'd get very excited if we found an old bolt that had hardly seen the light of day, so much the better if it was faded at the edges." They made suits inspired by Nudie, the Hollywood maven of rhinestones and Western-style jet-beaded tailoring, and also turned to Britain's heritage by utilizing floral-patterned William Morris fabrics sold by Liberty's.

Under the trademark "Hapshash and the Colored Coat," Waymouth and Michael English became London's genies of psychedelic art, designing graphics for UFO—the Unlimited Freak Out, a total-environment pavilion. "They are cool, polite, and very beautiful to look at," London's *Observer* described Waymouth and English in 1967, "with Harpo hairstyles, un-ironed marbled shirts, tight trousers, loose belts, and two-toned Cuban boots." Their day-glow graphics drew upon source material as diverse as Alphonse Mucha, Max Ernst, René Magritte, Hieronymous Bosch, William Blake, popular engravings of American Indians, Walt Disney, Edmund Dulac, ancient illustrations for treatises on alchemy, and contemporary comic books,

Granny Takes a Trip, London

Nigel Waymouth

145

all "boiled down to make a visionary and hallucinatory bouillabaisse," the *Observer* reported.

Waymouth designed a similar *mise en scène* for Granny's, engineering mind-expanding sleights of hand across the store's facade by regularly overhauling it between the closing of one work day and the opening of the next. Blown-up portraits of the scarred visages of American Indian braves might be replaced by the pouting moue of Jean Harlow splashed across the storefront. They had title to the space's forecourt as well, and so were able once to install an entire automobile body surging out of the front display window. Waymouth and his brethren saw themselves as soulmates of Ken Kesey's Merry Pranksters, the prototypical San Francisco acid heads, believing "you can change people's attitudes by playing nice games like that."

"There is a certain streak of fascism in people who are conservatively dressed," Michael Fish postulated in 1968. Two years earlier, he had opened Mr. Fish, cheek by jowl with London's Savile Row and its exclusive fleet of "gentleman's outfitters and haberdashers," as patrician menswear shops were traditionally known in London. Christening his boutique with his surname affixed to *Mister*, Fish spoofed the stately emporiums in which he had toiled for the prior decade; according to the old code, "you never went in a shop and called the salesman Peter or Fred." Traditionally, familiarity between customer and salesman was discouraged. Yet in the convention-smashing '60s, "Michael Fish, completely straightforward London suburb

Interior of Mr. Fish

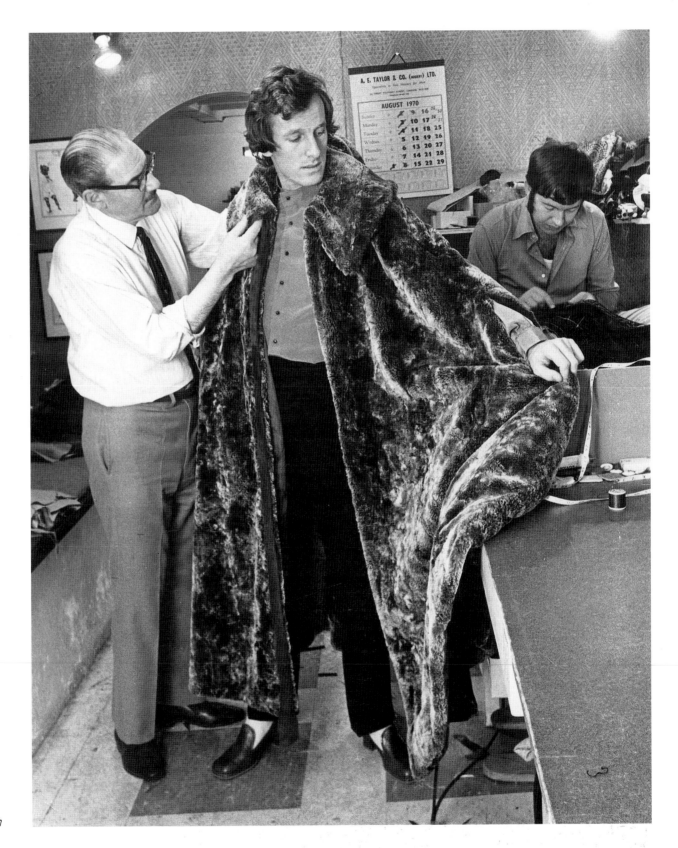

Michael Fish

147

working class, could mix with the customers. Suddenly there was a feeling of: 'Let's celebrate slightly that we're alive, the war's over, rationing's finished, and isn't color wonderful?'" Fish attributes his success to men's newly manifested desire to "wear fancy shirts to parties, *not* cheap ones from Carnaby Street—not that I'm knocking Carnaby Street. It was brilliant for the kids. Why John Stephen wasn't given a knighthood, or something even grander, I'll never know. But he was Scottish and he wasn't part of the English old boy network."

Carrying a rolled umbrella and a bowler hat to work, Fish had become an apprentice at age fifteen in a firm on Jermyn Street, the lane across Piccadilly from Savile Row that was the purlieu of elite shirtmakers. He learned the predilection of the aristocracy for "high quality: fine stitches, fine fabric, but not at outrageous prices, because the English upper class has never been keen on spending money unwisely—that's why they have leather patches on their jackets." After moving to New & Lingwood, haberdashers, he began attracting a following among offspring of the English nobs, for the firm functioned by appointment to Eton College. Undergraduate Etonians would customarily shop by consulting the same checklist their governess had given them as children. But as they came of age, "they didn't have to please Daddy anymore; they didn't have to please the trustees. They were interested in wearing something which was, if you like—fashionable." Following fashion trends has always been suspect in England, Fish notes, construed as a betrayal of the requisite detachment of the English aristocracy: "Royalty must never be fashionable."

After entering its hallowed doors in 1962, Fish become known as "the man who turned on Turnbull & Asser." He began as necktie buyer, ordering ties that were slowly growing wider and brighter in a swing away from the "Slim Jims" of the '50s. Wide ties soon became known in England as "kippers." "Make no bones about it, kipper was a pun on my name," Fish claims. "Wide ties had been there for ever, of course, as had lifebelts before Mae West, and the Homburg before it was called an Anthony Eden. The press needs to bitch against anything new, and the rudest name they could come up with is kipper—a smelly little fish with lots of tiny bones—very English, and quite delicious though."

His responsibilities at Turnbull & Asser multiplied. As ombudsman for the dressing gown department, he dispensed Indian silks in flamboyant colors, snatched up by upper-class squires who would caution Fish: "Don't tell anyone I bought that." Eventually, Fish supplied evening shirts—frilly, multicolored, in sheer silk or voile—in response to requests by debonair young men who wanted relief from the orthodoxy of the white dress shirt.

"Michael Fish and [partner] Barry Sainsbury are attempting to bridge the gap between Carnaby Street and Savile Row," the London *Sunday Times* reported after Fish struck out on

(RIGHT) Rudolf Nureyev with actress Monique Van
Voohren at New York's Arthur discotheque in 1965

(FAR RIGHT) Cartoon jacket, London

his own in 1966. Mr. Fish resembled a Mayfair drawing room, warmed by log fires, swagged
walls, flush with mahogany paneling and plush carpets. The merchandise was off-handedly
scattered across tables. Cashmere socks, sweaters, scarves, and sweater-robes beckoned.
Fish sold at-home lounging pajamas in exotic silk prints, and opulent dressing gowns. "Our
customers are very secure people," Mr. Fish explained, indicating bolts of orange, pink, and
purple crêpes earmarked for cossack and polo-neck shirts, "not the sort of man to be put off
by what his wife or boss says." Suits at Mr. Fish, available completely made-to-measure or
granted one fitting, were double-breasted, deep vented, featuring colorful linings and original
seaming details courtesy of a Turnbull & Asser cutter he had commandeered.

Declaring his contempt for "pedantic clothes," Fish explained that "Fashion is important
to me as a form of anarchy. The message is, don't allow yourself to be told what to wear or
how to act by others. If you do, the system will swallow you."

"You are going to see some slightly strange boys and girls," Pierre Cardin's voice intoned with
seductive omnipotence during his Paris couture showing in July 1966. Following this welcome,
Cardin surrendered the loudspeaker to a soundtrack of ambient sounds: jungle-bird cries succeeded by splintered notes and ominous clanks and thumps. Through his showroom sprinted
a squadron of helmeted young men and women, resembling outer-space or undersea explor-

Pierre Cardin with model in marmot fur jacket, 1966

ers. The women's skeletal skirts dangled from suspender ends or a thonglike collar buttoned over turtleneck sweaters. Their male counterparts zipped sleeveless jackets over matching turtleneck sweaters—bright red, purple, black. Cardin's "Cosmonauts" were the latest contribution to reciprocal dressing made by the most famous name in menswear during the '60s.

Cardin was a rara avis among the top drawer of Paris couturiers during the '60s, for his menswear achieved more commercial success than his women's. His couture collections, it often seemed, were offered as rhetorical exercises as much as mercantile endeavors. "Cardin's performance as a dress designer . . . has been low in concrete direct results," G. H. Dryansky wrote in *WWD* in 1975. "He has never influenced the look of the streets to anything like the extent of Courrèges in his heyday or Yves Saint Laurent." Cardin was a master entrepreneur to whom fashion often seemed an ancillary interest. "The history of fashion shows that couturiers merely concretize, each in his own manner, the taste of their times," Cardin said in 1967. With Iris Clert, doyenne of a Paris art gallery, he opened a night club, and Cardin built a new theater—L'Espace—to shelter avant-garde performance in Paris. Handsome and opinionated, Cardin was the consummate merchandiser, licensing his name to sundry franchised enterprises.

Raised in Italy by French parents, Pierre Cardin set out at seventeen for Vichy, then capital of occupied France. He apprenticed with a men's tailor, and made suits for a few private women clients. After reaching Paris, he worked for Paquin, Schiaparelli, and Dior, witnessing the birth pangs of Dior's New Look. In 1950, Cardin set up his shingle as a *costumier*, drafting *pièces d'occasion* for the masquerade balls that were the rage in Paris at the time, while establishing a reputation as one of the foremost women's suitmakers in Paris. By the mid-1950s he was installed in an eighteenth-century *hôtel particulier* on the fashionable Rue Saint-Honoré. He divided the mansion's first story into two boutiques, one called "Adam," the other "Eve." He supplied Adam with sweaters, vests, tapered shirts, and splashy ties. In the summer of 1957 he decided to incarnate himself as a full-blown couturier, and presented his first complete collection of women's clothing. Whereas Dior's architecture was rooted in a hypertrophied configuration of the female body, Cardin was an intrepid explorer of Euclidean and botanic abstractions. "For me fabric is nearly secondary. I believe first in shape, architecture, the geometry . . . of a dress." His "corolle" collars were extraordinary three-dimensional floral constructions; Cardin was the most sculptural of Paris couturiers. Yet by Janaury 1965, he concluded that "Modern haute couture clothes should look like rags on hangers. . . . Buyers are quite wrong when they think the opposite. That was right ten years ago. Now clothes are fluid and the body shapes them." Cardin was a pioneer in the use of cutouts, of virtuoso exercises in pleating, and appliqués that substituted for jewelry. He frequently included the most outlandish space-age garb, but was also, Gloria Emerson claimed in 1966, "a big leap ahead of anyone else when it comes to creating young-looking clothes that, oddly enough, often look great on quite grown-up women."

The axle of his collections was Japanese model Hiroko, whom he discovered modeling in a Tokyo department store. The Orient inspired Cardin "in a thousand different ways," he said. "Though I see it through Paris eyes, the impact on my fashion thinking is tremendous." Japanese motifs in Cardin's collections included characteristic brocades and lamés, as well as fabrics woven or printed with the elliptical distillations of Oriental landscapes.

In 1958, Cardin debuted a custom-order menswear collection in a show at the Hôtel Crillon in Paris. In contrast to the boxy suits of the period, he advanced a more body-conscious

Togetherness

look specifically designed to appeal to young men. Cardin's premiere collection was, accordingly, modeled on the rangy figures of university students. In 1961, the designer introduced a ready-to-wear line based on his original collection. Six years later, two-thirds of Cardin's annual gross of $22 million came from his male line, which now included suits, shirts, and ties, lounging pajamas, shoes, jewelry, fur coats, and leather suits.

"The job of fashion is not just to make pretty suits or dresses," Cardin avowed. "It is to change the face of the world by cut and line. It is to make another aspect of men evident."

Every staple of men's wear was assailed during the late '60s, the most sacrosanct being the necktie, for which scarves were proposed as replacements. In 1967, Cardin declared mandatory neckties "a very bourgeois idea. Have you ever heard of a Roman emperor wearing a tie? . . . It never happened in France until the 17th century anyway. . . . Now ties should be dropped." In place of the button-down shirt and tie, turtlenecks also became an option for informal evenings out. By Christmas 1967, Manhattan stores were reporting land office rushes on the turtleneck, although most merchants took a dubious view of the new fashion. "We will not go along with this evening business," harrumphed a spokesman for Brooks Brothers.

Capitalizing on the new parameters of masculinity, English Boy Ltd. opened in London in 1967 above the *haute bohême* boutique Quorum in Chelsea. The agency's aim, wrote Gloria Emerson, was "to annihilate all the clean-cut models now working." In opposition to the rugged stereotype then still ubiquitous in British advertising, the English Boys stable of models looked "too thin, morbid, and somehow suggest uncertainty of how much money they have in the bank."

Doomsayers predicted a neutralizing of procreative electricity, but the new reciprocity between the personas of men and women stimulated a depolarization rather than a dampening of erotic appeal. Men's cultivation of the aesthetic, decorative, "feminine" strains in their personality was erotically exciting to women. In 1968, at Saint Laurent's women's boutique in St. Tropez, young blades were buying his wide-leg pants and wearing them for themselves. "And the ironic thing," *WWD* observed, "is the young men who look most fragile and unmas-

Patterned knits and suede-and-jersey appliqués, from Stephen Burrows, late '60s

culine—are the ones who get all the girls." The '60s proposed that camaraderie, as much as positive/negative attraction, could exist between the sexes. "After twenty-five hundred years of lonely separation, they can once again share their experiences," Marshall McLuhan wrote in 1968. "Likeness in men's and women's dress . . . is terribly healthy," *WWD* had reassured its readers in 1966. "It's a symptom of liking each other. They've stopped worrying and their sick preoccupation with virility."

A dramatic litmus test of men's new attention to their appearance was hair, which men started growing with abandon. "When I look back at May, a solid month of social goings-on," Eugenia Sheppard dispatched in 1968, "all I can think of is a sea of luxuriant hair, soft, sometimes wavy, curling poetically around the collar and even slightly bouffant at the sides. I'm not talking about women's hair-dos." Outside of metropolitan capitals, long hair was a provocative sign language for dissidence, in which an extra inch could push the wearer's image

156

from conformity to subversion. At a precipitate rate, however, fine-feathered men in major cities flouted all sanctions against hair length or style.

The most shocking solecism remained the possibility that men might renounce bifurcated garments. Morrocan caftans eventually became somewhat acceptable by society-at-large, while bonafide skirts for men were frequently proposed but were never integrated into the mainstream. Proponents of draped rather than tailored clothes for men executed semantic tap dances to win acceptance for their ideas. "There's nothing new about the idea," Elizabeth Hawes remarked in 1967. "The Moroccans, the Arabs, and the Greeks have been at it for years, not to mention the Scots. The only time men blanche is when you call it a skirt. If you say kilt, it's all right."

"I've always believed men are not physically designed for trousers," Michael Fish says today. At the end of the '60s, he showed an elongated smoking jacket that raised eyebrows when it made a runway appearance at a charity event. Fish pontificated then: "Throughout history, the most virile of men have worn skirts or robes, but now people insist on clinging to their trousers, which are a Victorian invention that goes with a rigid mind. . . . Fashion, you see, is in the mind. You have to think differently before you can dress differently. By changing their clothes, people risk changing their whole lives and they are frightened."

THE
MEDIA

A priori assumptions of fashion journalism were shattered during the '60s. The monolithic autocracy of the fashion media began dancing to the new tunes of timeliness and relevance. The careering speed and unprecedented decentralization of taste-making left many journalists breathless. "Ten years ago fashion writers could still command: 'hems *will* be shorter; waists are *out*,'" Brigid Keenan of England's *Nova* magazine recalled in 1968. "Now we hardly dare predict past the middle of next week."

The war chests of advertising's bounty, which seemed bottomless at the high noon of the '60s, made possible an unprecedented lavishness in the transatlantic fashion glossies. In their pages, clothing was used as one ingredient in the fabrication of exotic visions lifted from the Arabian nights. Diana Vreeland was the most powerful of Merlins summoning these chimeras across the slick pages of fashion magazines. High priestess of fashion magazine editors, Vreeland became American *Vogue*'s editor-in-chief in 1962 after a twenty-five year association with *Harper's Bazaar*. Infatuated with youth, Vreeland propelled her magazine toward a fantasy kingdom where the latest trends were eagerly embraced, albeit one beat after they'd been exposed by the junior fashion magazines. Vreeland's pages provoked furors from advertisers and audiences who groused that clothes were accessorized for maximum theatrical impact, and therefore made inaccessible to the consumer. Yet *Vogue*'s status as entertainment as much as diagrammatic instruction made possible its singular glory during Vreeland's reign.

Vreeland styled herself as a somewhat overripe embodiment of the quintessential fashion magazine matriarch. Her anthracite hair and sinuous stride were starkly arresting and frankly affected. Her court resounded with edicts as capricious as the monarch's tastes. At *Vogue*, remembers Kezia Keeble, "things were not allowed to be called outfits or ensembles—they were 'turn-outs.'" "I'm not always *right*!" Vreeland warned, but few of her ladies-in-waiting dared contradict her. Vreeland's memos were cherished for their apothegms on taste and style: "In this hour of gold galoon," she cautioned at the height of the "rich hippie" embellishment, "let us not forget one black pearl or the Niarchos diamond."

"As editors in those days," recalls Kezia Keeble, "we did not shop the market to find clothes; we went into the market with ideas and told the designers what to do." The photo portfolios that resounded with the greatest impact were often shot using clothes made especially for the photo session. Joan Sibley recalls *Vogue*'s Polly Allen Mellon phoning in 1968, "asking for something special" for an Avedon shoot she was planning for Jean Shrimpton and Julie Christie. Mellon arrived with a sheaf of vintage drawings by Erté, whose fantasias of the early '20s recorded handkerchief-point sleeves anticipating those sweeping fashion in the late '60s. Inspired by the illustrations, the two designers developed a heavy linen blouse with enor-

Model Deborah Dixon, photographed by Emeric Bronson in Barcelona's Parco Guell, 1964

Diana Vreeland insisted on "Youthful breasts, nipples pointing skyward!" for sketches to accompany the biannual Vogue seminar, which the magazine used to broadcast its fashion message to the design community. Illustrator Maning caught Vreeland as she collared an in-house messenger at Condé Nast to demonstrate her ideal.

mous pleated sleeves. Because of the fabric's intractability, "we had to send the linen out to be mechanically pleated by having it steamed between paper," recalls Sibley. "We cut and basted the linen with the paper still pressed between the folds. It was a lot of work, and just for the photograph—one wearing and the pleats were out. (After that we produced the blouse in crêpe.) But we wound up with six pages [in the August 1968 issue]."

"The paradox of *Vogue* in those years," writes Clara Pierre in 1976's *Looking Good*, "was that underneath the mod veneer . . . there remained the same old symbiotic dependence on the couture houses." For the glossies were no less addicted to flummery than in previous decades. They remained mortgaged not only to the increasingly exhausted couture mystique, but to the titanic merchandisers of Seventh Avenue. Fashion magazines ran page after page of glorious models dressing up "musts": run-of-the-mill merchandise displayed because of the incestuous relationship between the advertising and editorial departments of fashion magazines.

Very young and beautiful, Caterine Milinaire was *au fait* with the circuit-breakers of the Establishment, but a champion of the untried. Milinaire blazed a superb path through the fashion media of the '60s. She grew up in France, the daughter of a painter and of one of television's first female producers. After her mother's second marriage, to England's duke of Bedford,

Solarization was a popular photographic technique exploited during the '60s.

Cheap Chic, a seminal alternative fashion handbook. Today, she produces video documentaries, the culmination of a long-standing interest in photography. A self-professed "documentist and student of life," Milinaire eventually became disenchanted with *Vogue*'s ornate aesthetic. "I didn't wear much make-up, and so I didn't like the models wearing a lot, either, nor having their hair too twisted. Mrs. Vreeland would always say, 'Take this to the hairdresser and do something with the hair.' I'd tell her: 'Well, I just like people to look natural.' Finally she exclaimed, 'But, *Caterine*, don't you understand?! Natural is boring! Artifice is what fashion is

Early in the '60s, Caterine Milinaire modeled Louis Feraud's couture clothes at Woburn Abbey, her stepfather's castle in Britain.

all about.' Suddenly something really clicked in my mind," Milinaire remembers. "I understood that fashion journalism kind of went against everything that I like. I'm not about artifice, and the industry cannot exist without pulls and tucks and ribbons. I realized eventually that it was *not* my medium, really."

The sanctums of press lords were not exempt from the panic and disorientation that the '60s engendered in conservative quarters. Felicity Green recalls a confrontation with the chairman of London's *Mirror* newspaper group, "a very austere man who kept a very respectable distance between him and his work force." "Why do you keep putting that Mary Quant rubbish in our papers?" he challenged Green. "I believe it's fun and I think it's going to be important," she replied. "Do you?" the newspaper baron demanded. "What will you do to me if I continue to put it in?" Green asked flippantly. "'I should probably fire you,' he told me. But he didn't— when you're faced with a tidal wave, you go with it."

An editorial slant that focused on the frontiers of experimental clothing elicited the censure of Charlotte Curtis, editor of "Women's News" at the *New York Times*. Patricia Peterson, fashion editor for the *Times*, remembers frequently locking horns with Curtis. "When are you going to get real clothes for real women, Pat?" she demanded. "I told her I wasn't here to work as a consumer service, but to show what's happening in fashion, to report news." "These things are only for kids," Curtis complained. "Well, it depends on your body," Peterson rejoined. "The point is that it's happening, so take it as news. Do you want people to look back on the archives of the *Times* and not find it registered?"

The power broker of the American fashion media was public relations officer Eleanor Lambert. It was reported that when a prospective client had once asked her what she could do for his company, Lambert had replied: "I own every fashion editor in America." While the incident may be apocryphal, Lambert did have a deathgrip on the brass rings bestowed by the fashion oligarchy. She presided over the annual Coty awards as well as the best-dressed poll. In 1943, while leading the New York Couture Group, she had organized a biannual press week, at which national editors were flown to New York and spoon-fed the party line for country-wide dissemination. Dissenters faced excommunication. "[Geoffrey] Beene and [Bill] Blass are dear sweet fellows and they do some nice clothes, but how long are we expected to go on doing puff profiles on all of them?" queried Eleanor Nangle of the Chicago *Tribune*, one of the few editors who dared defy Lambert's electioneering.

America's most famed columnist was Eugenia Sheppard, who penned a daily column, "Inside Fashion," for the *Herald Tribune* and syndicated newspapers around the country.

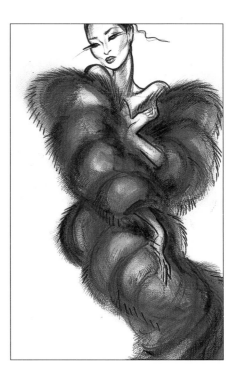

China Machado, a top model of the early '60s, became a fashion editor at Harper's Bazaar *later in the decade.*

Nguyen Khanh with Patricia Peterson of the New York Times

"Her fashion column . . . commands as much attention on Seventh Avenue as do the political columns of James Reston and Walter Lippmann on Capitol Hill," noted Lewis H. Lapham in the *Saturday Evening Post.* Sheppard's viewpoint was engagingly benign but nonetheless entangled by her allegiances within the industry. She blended small-town horse sense with urbane savoir faire. When Peggy Moffitt modeled Gernreich's transparent blouse in 1964, many in the audience gasped, while "Miss Sheppard, a hardened reporter before whom even a French designer has trembled, remained impassive," Lapham reported. "It's very square to wear a bra with Rudi's clothes," was Sheppard's pronouncement. Betsey Johnson, to whom Eugenia Sheppard dedicated a column early in the designer's career, recalls: "She didn't understand my work, but she was open-minded, *joyful*, warm, unthreatened."

Sheppard appeared to collude with John Fairchild, publisher of *Women's Wear Daily*, for they shared a relentless fixation on the moves and mores of the fashion-conscious upper class. Sheppard's and Fairchild's unceasing coverage elevated the Beautiful People to a new celebrity class. Diana Vreeland, too, summoned the denizens of *Debrett's Peerage* and the *Almonoch de Gotha*—and their American counterparts—to make guest appearances in her pages.

Vreeland denied, however, that the paramount credential of her favorites was wealth. "We mean people who are beautiful to look at," she insisted. "It's been taken up to mean people who are rich. We mean the charmers but there is no harm to be rich."

Fairchild, who took command of his family's newspaper in 1960, turned it from an obscure industry news sheet into a caustic, controversial arbiter. *WWD* genuflected before those it admired and denounced acerbically those who did not make its grade. *WWD* invented its own piquant jargon, freely employing fashion's ability to appropriate the specialized nomenclature of more solemn disciplines. Typically, the newspaper commented in 1967 that Gloria Vanderbilt had always been "a Fashion Conservative—strictly understated couture, but now she's a Fashion Liberal—more daring and willing to experiment by adapting Today's look to herself."

Richard Avedon (seated, in horn rims), in the midst of the fashion press assembled at a 1967 Gernreich show, watches a model display a linen dress and headband.

Mary Peacock and Blair Sabol during their stewardship *of* Rags

WWD brandished many different taglines and respective points of view, yet its concerted sentiments were royalist at heart. In concord with the egalitarian tenor of the late '60s, it impugned smug conformity and label dropping. Yet it was Mrs. William Paley, walking down Fifth Avenue in a plain black turtleneck and shirt, whom it said provided incontrovertible evidence in 1968 that "The Day of the Status Symbol is Dead."

"There weren't any journalistic standards in fashion at the time," Mary Peacock believes. A founder of *Ms.* magazine and former fashion editor of the *Village Voice*, Peacock kicked off *Rags*, a heterodox fashion journal, at the end of the '60s. The newspaper's editorial consultant was Blair Sabol, the voice of "Outside Fashion" at the *Village Voice*. "Outside Fashion," which Sabol and Stephanie Harrington began in 1967, turned the tables on Sheppard's constituency. "Blair was one of the first ones to say 'Excuse me, this emperor doesn't have any clothes on,'" Peacock recalls. Sabol tilted her lance against the lords of Seventh Avenue, complaining that "The fashion establishment is perhaps more entrenched than even the political one."

The *cri du coeur* sounded by *Rags* was "the acknowledgement of personal, individual style," Peacock states. "There needed to be a magazine that reported what people were actually wearing, because that was what was most interesting. We wanted to define fashion as everybody's individual statement. The combat boots and torn jeans and rock band T-shirt is *not* anti-fashion; it's just that person's fashion.

Fashion magazines dropped anchor at far-flung ports of call in their search for sumptuous backdrops for location shots.

170

"Blair covered standard fashion from the outsider's viewpoint. We were pushing it another step, which was to say 'it's not even so important what *they're* doing.' Fashion on the street was where it really was at. We didn't feel we had to go to the shows—for what? If we wanted to know what was there we could pick up *Vogue*, and that was fine, too. We were just saying there's more to it.

"I've been told by many—Condé Nast editors among others—that what we started in *Rags* influenced them enormously," Peacock avows. "They would have gotten there eventually; it's just that we were first."

The '60s had seen a marvelous eclecticism stretch the supercilious purviews of the fashion media to accommodate the agitations of groups that had formerly been peripheral. But the efflorescence of the '60s would not long outlive the decade. An editor remembers suggesting in 1971 to the newly installed chief of one of the world's most venerable fashion bibles that the magazine publish a fashion feature on Tina Turner. "I'd written a memo and I said '*Please* . . . she does these extraordinary whip-like dances, her skin is so beautiful, she is just incredible' and on and on. I even thought I could get Seventh Avenue to actually produce some of these clothes, and they'd be called 'Tiny Tina Turn-ons.'" The young editor delivered the memo to her superior, who "looked and said 'Oh—she's black?'" The story progressed no further.

THE MODELS

"Children always want to be like the others, and so it used to bother me terribly that I wasn't," famed fashion model Veruschka said in 1967. "Later on, I found out it's not so bad to be different." Renowned for her unique appearance and photographic impact, Veruschka was one of the great models of the '60s who revised the traditional ethos of the fashion model. They forfeited the model's erstwhile position as idealized composites of their audience's aspirations. Instead, they elucidated the doctrine of fashion as self-expression by projecting personas so distinctive that identification or imitation by the viewer was often impossible. In the '60s, "models were not pretty, the way we think of them today. Rather, they were extraordinary," write Robin Rolmach Lakoff and Racquel L. Scherr in *Face Value: The Politics of Beauty*.

"They were real personalities more than almost any models before or since," says Mary Peacock, currently Editor-in-Chief of *Model* magazine. The new power of the model to create her own image contributed to the ongoing upset of fashion's hierarchy. "Fashion models have changed subtly in the last couple of years," Brigid Keenan assessed in 1968. "Their old function was simply to make clothes look so desirable that the reader immediately wanted to imitate them by buying those clothes. Nowadays you might be forgiven for thinking that sometimes the only promoting is of themselves."

Veruschka, standard-bearer for the new breed of fashion model, used her trade for the exploration of private fantasies. Veruschka was "the only model," in hair stylist Ara Gallant's experience, "whose opinion of how she should look, and how the photograph should be, is a prime consideration." Roaming the world with photographer/consort Franco Rubartelli, Veruschka dispatched field reports documenting her metamorphosis into an infinity of bizarre apparitions. She redefined the fashion model as an intrepid explorer on the cutting edge of thought about appearance and adornment. "Modelling had always been glamorous," wrote Andy Warhol in *The Pop Sixties*, "but now it could be outrageous, too."

Veruschka was a German countess whose father was executed in 1943 for his participation in a conspiracy to assassinate Hitler. Raised in a succession of European refugee camps, Veruschka learned early in life to see herself as an outsider. Her six-foot-tall adult presence was a curious blend of blazing physical strength and withdrawn introspection. The sun ardently flattered her leonine tresses and freckled Alpine complexion. Her eyes were an enchanting cornflower blue, her power-packed body glowed with the disciplined vigor of a Valkyrie. But an enigma was refracted in the curiously craggy planes of Veruchka's face. Her eyes were drawn irresistibly to the most remote frontier ever embraced by the fashion glossies. The clothes she wore became stepping stones to a visionary landscape that was sometimes scabrous and grotesque, sometimes as luscious as the mythical Cythera—sacred pleasance of Venus.

Lauren Hutton in a blistered Moroccan cloth jumpsuit, a rage in 1966

Veruschka in the Sahara, where she teamed with designer Giorgio Sant' Angelo to devise to a series of nomadic tableaus.

Richard Avedon photographs Veruschka in 1968.

Veruschka inhabited a Felliniesque spectrum that stretched beyond the stock catalogue of stereotypes in which most models were imprisoned. She shuttled to the dark side of the moon; she prowled through primeval jungles; she floated serenely through the portals of ancient citadels. Veruschka soared to the empyrean, but she could never escape a splendid yet haunted isolation. "She'll let you look into her dream," observed Richard Avedon, "but she wouldn't fit in yours."

"Her features were so clear and uncrowded that, depending on her make-up, she could appear to be anything she chose—even Oriental," recalled Dorien Leigh, a legendary model of the '40s and '50s, who became a model's agent. Veruschka's age, her class, her race all became mercurial variables; she used make-up as an agent of camouflage and transformation as much as conventional beautification.

Veruschka's looks were airtight. They were not designed for easy access and maximum intelligibility. Her rites of posture and impersonation were too abstruse to serve as how-to blueprints. She subverted the instructional relationship prevailing between the fashion photograph and reader; she confounded the model's customary function as glamorized saleswoman. Veruschka prosletyzed not so much on behalf of a specific line or outfit but in celebration of the eternal allure of self-transcendence offered by the ritual of fashion.

Jean Shrimpton was the *belle idéale* of '60s modeling. In the early part of her career, Shrimpton, in contrast to many other great models of the decade, did inspire widespread imitation. Her swinging curtain of hair and starflower-lashed eyes were zealously copied, for she was idolized as a personification of London's renaissance. Professionally, she incarnated a magnum embodiment of the racy, insouciant spirit of Mod. "She is a perfect heroine for us," Alexander Plunket Greene said in 1965. Lithe, fair, and fleet, Shrimpton oscillated with the promise and freedom of youth. A poetic English rose, she married London sophistication to the rustic fragrance of English pastoral drama.

Shrimpton was a transitional figure between the old and new fashion-model mythologies. She became the world's foremost fashion model under the tutelage of photographer David Bailey. Personally and professionally intertwined, their Pygmalian/Galatea relationship freshly endowed the image of the fashion photographer with a Lothario's lusty swagger. "He made me exactly what he wanted me to be," Shrimpton recounted in 1980. "I was his fantasy come to life—which eventually became very hard to take." Yet Shrimpton was a catalyst as much as a vessel. "In her wonderfully quiet English way she had a tremendous sense of herself," recalls Frances Patiky Stein, who edited Shrimpton and Bailey's work for *Glamour*. In 1981,

(*Left*) *Jean Shrimpton and David Bailey announce their engagement in December 1963.*

(*Opposite*) *An August 1965 day in the life of Jean Shrimpton, modeling the Paris collections before Richard Avedon's camera for American* Harper's Bazaar.

Bailey's chum, photographer Lord Patrick Lichfield, posed the "debatable question as to who made whom famous."

Of Shrimpton and Bailey's collaboration, Kennedy Fraser wrote: "The image they have wrought lies deep within each follower of fashion." The photographs that first brought them international attention threw a monkey wrench into the relentlessly upper-class indoctrination of the previous decade's models. Shrimpton's dégagé charm mitigated against the impeccable polish of '50s couture. Shrimpton instead suggested links to antiestablishment elements that had not yet infiltrated the elite precincts of the couture. She synthesized Audrey Hepburn's

McCabe. Avedon's photos of Luna's sinewy, spidery limbs, cobra-shaped face, and hermetic poise evoked thunderclaps of attention, and the model enjoyed a windfall of employment. "Back in Detroit I wasn't considered beautiful or anything," she said in Paris in 1966. "But here I'm different." *Paris Match* had just published a portfolio containing eleven different photographers' views of Luna; later in the year she modeled the couture collection for British *Vogue* and appeared in William Klein's *Qui Etes-Vous Polly McGoo*, a satire of the fashion industry. On the way to international notoriety, Luna had exorcised her past, at least externally. She conjured a persona that was not confined to what the camera recorded. "Her speech related to no one else's at all," recalls photographer Emeric Bronson. "She spoke not with a broad *A* or a French *R*, but in an accent that she'd invented. I had an assistant, a very bright fellow, a real Yankee from New England. One day we came across Donyale on the street, and after leaving her he asked me: "Is she a countess?"

Pat Ast, an outrageous model of the late '60s, claimed she was the first large-size model to parade down a high-fashion runway. Here she cavorts with Penelope Tree and Halston in the designer's salon.

As the teenager wielded greater cultural and economic power, she, too, became one of the former "minorities" admitted into the high-fashion magazines. Penelope Tree and Twiggy were seventeen and sixteen when their first photographs appeared in British and American *Vogue*. By March 1968, Twiggy and Tree were costars in a memorable Avedon portfolio lavishly printed in French and American *Vogue*, which showed "the Tree" and "the Twig" dancing through the spring couture collections. Dryads of the psychedelic age, they sprinted and frolicked with waiflike effervescence.

The backgrounds of the two young women were worlds apart. Tree was the daughter of British industrialist Ronald Tree, and of political powerhouse Marietta Peabody. Twiggy, née Leslie Hornby, was reared in a London suburb by parents of modest means. She became a heroine to working-class London teens, as well as the darling of récherché fashion editors, while Tree's appeal was more specifically to the cognoscenti. Young as they were, each projected a powerful and unique look. Twiggy's ethereal androgyny was the ultimate repudiation of the bosom-fixated '50s. Tree followed in Veruschka's steps by tendering her photographic masquerades as if through a glass darkly. Her expression was alternately cryptic and droll; her make-up a chalky film. "Her style is almost science," Jean Shrimpton declared of Tree's precisely calibrated artifice.

Tree starred in some of the most off-center editorials commissioned by Diana Vreeland. Before Avedon's lenses she impersonated Byzantine hierophants, mythic neriads, Ganymedes, and Rapunzels, all abetted by the wizardry of hairdresser/make-up artist Ara Gallant, who enjoyed teaming with Tree because she "loves to work along with me and there's a definite communication between us." Tree defended the obscurity of her sittings, which were guaranteed to alienate the magazine's upscale, over-thirty readers and its corporate advertisers. "You can't look like *Vogue*. It doesn't want you to," she explained in 1968. "It just wants to show you what individuality is."

"Are you ugly?" asked an ad in the Personal Columns of the London *Times*. It had been placed by the founders of Ugly's, a London modeling agency that recruited its charter stable of clients late in the decade. Cofounder Robin Wright explained: "What we mean by ugly is ugly in relation to the conventional Hollywood face." Fostering a "fresh respect for people as they are—warts and all—and a withering of the middle-class myths about Anglo-Saxon good looks" were high on Ugly's agenda, Gloria Emerson reported in the *New York Times* in 1969. Ugly's owners detected the new pulchritude in asymmetry celebrated by the '60s. "Because the faces of our models are more interesting, they are more beautiful." Robin Wright considered that the pub-

lic's recent acceptance of irregularity had in part been sowed by the new leaders of conventional modeling. Twiggy and Veruschka had advanced the cause of individuality, Wright claimed, for "they are both deviations from the classic English beauty type personified by Jean Shrimpton."

"Her person floats far above such terrestrial matters as sales," the *New Yorker*'s Kennedy Fraser wrote of Naomi Sims. "That she is black additionally frees many of her admirers from disaffected comparisons, and forestalls the notion that if they dieted or got their hair done they might in any way resemble her." As Sims ascended in the late '60s, radical chic was mobilizing the wealthy behind liberal causes, while modeling superstars were encouraged to be unique performers rather than templates for the masses of women. Sims's skin color was a tribute to the political correctness of her employers and a concomitant of the fashion gloss-

Twiggy, 1967: To Cecil Beaton, she was an Ariel of the electronic age.

Twiggy ahoy! Modeling a dress from the ready-to-wear collection she endorsed in 1967, accompanied by matching knee make-up.

Elsa Peretti modeled in the '60s while starting to
design her sensuous jewelry in semiprecious materials.

184

Naomi Sims modeling, for Vogue, *a pheasant feather vest from the Electric Circus boutique, and silk print pants bound with silk strips by Stephen Burrows*

Elsa Peretti with Giorgio Sant' Angelo, who *masterminded the* Scheherezade *ensemble in which she was enveloped*

ies' pursuit of the extraordinary. Yet it was far from the sum of her credentials. An exclamatory presence of grandeur and incandescence, Sims generated an amperage that "breaks through the printed page or television screen," Bernadine Morris reported in the *Times*, "and makes people shout Hurrah when she steps into a room."

"The person of Miss Sims is amply endowed with a kind of nerve-end understanding that life is often very sad," Fraser commented. Born and raised in Pittsburgh, Sims had never known her father, who was a porter. After her mother suffered a nervous breakdown, she was taken to live in a home for girls and a series of foster residences. Sims, who today markets a

Naomi Sims photographed for the cover of the New York Times *fashion supplement, August 1967, in a melton cloth cape by Daniel Hechter for Devonbrook*

line of cosmetics and wigs for black women, had been obsessed with fashion since childhood. She came to New York in 1966 to study merchandising at the Fashion Institute of Technology, supporting herself as an illustrator's model. In 1967, she made a spectacular catapult into photographic modeling when she appeared on the cover of the biannual fashion supplement of the *New York Times*. In 1968, Sims graced the cover of the *Ladies Home Journal*, the first black woman to appear on the cover of a major women's magazine. "Success is important to me because of my childhood," she said in 1968. "It gives me security. It's an obsession to become somebody and to be somebody really important."

In the wake of Dr. Martin Luther King's assassination in April 1968, a bevy of black models was absorbed into the advertising and editorial folds. Yet the specter of tokenism was far from faint. The desirability of black models hinged on a readily African look. "Do you know how they're working it on TV? You've got to be dark enough to come across as a Negro to get the job," an unidentified black model told *WWD* in 1968. "Since they're making the big gesture of using a Negro, they want it to be obvious." Furnishing the latest grist for fashion's novelty-hungry mill did little to salve an underlying insecurity. "'Oh, boy,' you say to yourself, 'that's lots of work coming our way.' But underneath there's still the feeling this isn't going to last."

"I considered myself an excellent skeleton on which to build the fantasies which made people dream," Benedetta Barzini declares. A beautiful and brilliant young woman fleeing a traumatic childhood passed in a prominent Italian family, Barzini arrived in New York in 1963 and became one of the most frequently showcased faces in the transatlanatic *Vogue*s. Barzini's features were "so remarkable that no make-up could possibly alter the way she looks," Naomi Sims reported in *How to Be a Top Model*, written in 1979 when Barzini was active in the women's movement in Italy. "She looks exactly the same with no make-up, in a plain skirt and sweater, as she did dressed by Givenchy in the pages of *Vogue*."

"I fell into it somehow by absolute chance, if not by mistake," Barzini recalls. Her father

After working for photographer Melvin Sokolsky, Ali MacGraw became a popular model for junior fashion magazines before making her screen debut in Goodbye, Columbus.

187

was author Luigi Barzini whose book *The Italians* was an American bestseller; her mother was a French globe-trotter. But Barzini lived independently from age fourteen; at nineteen, she was estranged from her family, studying art and theater in Milan. Editor Consuelo Crespi encountered her adventitiously and asked her to pose for Italian *Vogue*; that debut piqued Diana Vreeland's interest and elicited a summons to New York.

Modeling was a tolerable berth to shelter an identity in flux, a means to buy the time and independence needed to heal childhood wounds.

There were times—when I was heavily made up and wearing a superb evening dress—that I felt as though I were deep inside a fairy tale. There were other times when I'd really be sick. At four o'clock in the morning, doing the collections in Paris, I'd want to say: "Another dress— No!—no matter what it looks like."

But you tell yourself a story and you pull through. I would go in front of the lights and start the ball rolling. The photographer would tell me it was right, it was wrong, to do something else. It was creative when I could use my body to make a shape. That's what I liked best— searching for shapes, and interpreting the materials I had on. In a fur or a heavy coat I might imagine I was something elemental— a piece of a mountain or a stone, not simply a person walking down the street.

In many of the lushest sessions commissioned by the Vreeland ministry, Barzini's smoldering authority evoked the high promontories of an archaic Mediterranean civilization. Her onyx-colored eyes and hair made her perfect for the hothouse aesthetic of Vreeland editorials, but her complexion was too dark to appeal to the middle-American audience to which advertising

Benedetta Barzini, 1967

agencies targeted their pitches. Barzini remembers an executive in her modeling agency counseling her: "I've looked at your file, and, well, you're not making enough money. I also notice that you never come to my parties, and every six months I have to renew your working permit."

"The point of the conversation," Barzini sensed, "was that it would be ideal for me to marry an American citizen that could have been a client of the agency. There were always guys looking for models to marry and divorce and use them up in the process. It's merchandising. They were businessmen and they knew the potentials of a girl. Marrying the model of the moment would enhance their personal image. Lots of girls would be happy to be Mrs. X for awhile and lead a glamorous life—before going back to Mom in Norway and marrying a local man. 'It's no problem,' I was told. 'Divorces are easy.'"

Traversing the vertiginous pitfalls of a duplicitous world, she struggled to maintain her equilibrium. "My mother was very rich, and I knew my aim in life was not to fall into the trap of money—I called it 'falling into the honey jar.' Very often when I was working, I would think 'Yes, but my feet are dirty.' I didn't wash my feet"—a way for Barzini to keep hers on the ground. "I'm dressed as a goddess, but only I know I've got dirty feet."

"What I most enjoyed in New York was passing through this mix of different worlds, being able to leave Bobby Kennedy's birthday party and go downtown to an off-off Broadway situation." At Truman Capote's masked ball at the Plaza and at dinner parties on Fifth Avenue she observed high society's "big effort to reconstruct historical periods that didn't belong to them—French furniture, French tapestry—in a desperation to find an umbilical cord to Europe. That made me very appealing." At Warhol's Factory she watched the artist set in train "a hungry Polish boy's vengeance. Warhol knew exactly who he had around himself and how to turn people into slaves. He was only interested in people that were profoundly destroyed by the system, or had great talent." During one period, "on every weekend night Andy and I would be at the Balloon Farm downtown with our fingers in the oils working the psychedelic lights." Warhol's lieutenant, Gerard Malanga, was a swain who wrote a volume of *Poems for Benedetta*. Another admirer was Salvador Dali, who told "me I looked exactly like his wife had when they married. He had a wedding cake made, he had me dressed up the way Gala had been, and we posed for a wedding picture."

Barzini was one of the few who were admitted to the private sanctum of Jasper Johns. On Saturdays she would repair to his atelier to watch the artist at work. "I loved him. He had a great mind," she muses. "He was actually very simple. He came from the country, and he was not Manhattan. He was very genuine, very violent, in the sense that he wasn't mediating

189

Benedetta Barzini with Salvador Dali at their "wedding" in New York during the mid '60s. Barzini today is a Milanese journalist.

at all in his paintings, and very profound. He talked freely about why he had painted something that way, what he was into at that moment. He was not at all the bear he was in the public world."

Few in fashion aroused similar admiration; one who did was Irving Penn. "I loved Penn because he didn't try to hide his suffering and his ambivalence about fashion. I loved the simplicity of his studio. There was nothing ostentatious about it. There wasn't any music. He wasn't trying to be fashionable. Penn had feeling for people, independent of their beauty, or the fact that they were women or children or African. He wasn't effusive. He didn't try to get you turned on by telling you over and over how divine you were. I'd do something, and he might say, 'Perfect, let's get it straight now,' or 'You look empty. You can do better than that.'

(*ABOVE*) *The eyes were the focal point, and each top model devised her signature treatment of them: Cathy Dahmen, 1967.*

(*RIGHT*) *Pat Cleveland in Stephen Burrows's "rain forest" camouflage*

"I was told I couldn't model by every tacky editor and photographer in the world," Peggy Moffitt recalls. "I really had to buck it all, but I saw something else in it. The possibility of its being a new art form." As showroom and photographic model, and indispensable inspiration to Rudi Gernreich, Moffitt startled the fashion world with her Kabuki-inspired face-painting and her runway caperings. Moffitt used each outfit as the text of a cameo playlet, changing her walk and persona and interjecting wit and levity. In a Renaissance-accented dress, she fled across Gernreich's showroom emitting a silent scream à la Ophelia. Her *gestes* "either amuse or outrage audiences; in either case their reaction is convulsive," reported eyewitness Robert Riley in *The Fashion Makers*. Orchestrated by Moffitt, Gernreich's shows were unembellished by special lighting or soundtrack, yet they were nonetheless rated "without question . . . the

In 1964, Diana Vreeland began featuring seventeen-year-old Marisa Berenson, granddaughter of famed couturiere Elsa Schiaparelli, in the pages of her magazine.

most spectacular . . . in New York," by the *Daily News*. Moffitt was an original whose professional image was completely self-created. In her autobiography, Twiggy recalled that sharing a photo assignment with Moffitt was a revelation: "She designs shapes with her arms, her hands, the tilt of her head. . . . She consciously controlled the sort of shape she presented to the camera. . . . She taught me how much more a model puts in her work than just a face and body."

Today Moffitt lives in Los Angeles with her husband, photographer William Claxton, with whom she recorded a comprehensive documentation of Gernreich's oeuvre. Dance was her first love, and an abiding one. Talking on her terrace, overlooking the yawning panorama of the city, Moffitt admits that when asked about the '60s, she tends to go on automatic pilot; she'd much prefer discussing Moira Shearer and *The Red Shoes*. Moffitt grew up in Los Angeles, the daughter of screenwriter and film critic Jack Moffitt. As a teenager, she worked after school at the Beverly Hills Jax where, unbeknownst to her, she admired and sold clothes designed by Rudi Gernreich. The labels said only "Jax." She studied for two years at New York's Neighborhood Playhouse before returning to Los Angeles and beginning to model while acting in television and film.

"When somebody points a camera at me," Moffitt says today, "I feel a responsibility to do something. I want to hear that click. I found out very soon that the model, not the photographer, is the one who causes the click. I feel it is the model's responsibility to create that decisive moment."

Her self-direction arose out of necessity: "I had the great good fortune to do my first job with Bill, for an album cover he was shooting. He taught me everything I know about lighting my face. But then I worked with every schlock photographer on the face of the earth before being teamed with anybody that was pretty good. I used to go into people's studios and think: 'This is their palace, and I am a lump of clay that they should mold however they want to see me.' That produced stacks of the most rotten photographs you ever saw in your life. Then I realized that perhaps I should go in with *my* personality and *my* point of view. The moment I did that good things started happening. Once I saw that I could base modeling on my ability and my talent, the light flashed. But something that had to do with the accident of my birth—who can take a bow for that?"

In Gernreich she found a mentor who gave her her head. "The wonderful thing for me personally about Rudi was at last a cohort, a soulmate!" Gernreich extended her complete latitude in showing his clothes.

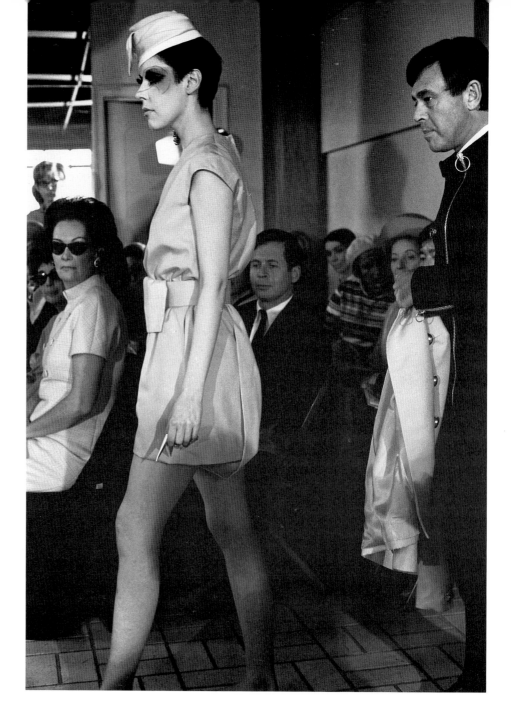

Peggy Moffitt models an organge silk shantung dress with hot pink panel, styled after a Siamese panung, at a Gernreich show in November 1967. The silk hat is blue. The finger guards are lacquered paper.

We thought so much alike. I remember an entire group of one collection was Siamese-inspired. Without knowing anything about what he was doing, I'd been working on a make-up that was completely of that spirit. It could not have been worn with a suit—it was like a great tatoo around my eyes. I looked at these clothes, and said "Well, I've been working on this make-up—Would you like me to use that?"

We were so much on the same wavelength that he used to walk into my apartment in New York and ask: "Where did you get that potholder? Downstairs at the department store," I'd say, and then find out that he'd bought the same one in Beverly Hills.

194

Erudite and opinionated, Moffitt conceived her work by drawing upon a dossier of observation and exposure. She used "every museum I walked into, every picture of Nijinsky I looked at, every experience down to just walking down the street and seeing how people behave toward each other."

Moffitt applied the most starkly opaque facade of the '60s. Her face-painting was in direct contrast to the pale lipped, blush-cheeked "natural" countenance sculpted by Shrimpton and ubiquitous throughout the decade. In Moffit's color scheme, neon orange eyelids might be silhouetted against a rice-paper foundation. Her fantasy make-up would seem anomolous until the late '60s, when the hallucinogenic war paint of the hippies spurred a widespread urge to paint the face as if it were a canvas.

Moffitt did not apply her maquillage thinking "'I don't want anybody to see me.' I did it in terms of design, but within that design it did allow me to tell the truth—to create something. There is a wonderful Oriental proverb that goes something like 'Show me a man with a mask and I'll show you a man who tells the truth.' A mask does allow you that freedom. If you hide your identity, then you can be or say anything you want. You get a terrorist on TV, they scramble the image, and then he tells us all.

"One thing I didn't like much about acting was the possibility that people would assume that my role was what I was like in reality." Likewise, she emphasizes, "I wanted modeling to be a performance."

ROCK AND POP

"What are you wearing to Janis's concert?" asked an advertisement placed by the Manhattan boutique Abracadabra. It was a week before Janis Joplin's appearance at Madison Square Garden in December 1969. In the *Village Voice* Abracadabra printed a rundown of fifty suggestions beginning with "velvet gaucho pants" and ending with "oversized fringe stoles." At the concert itself, the singer ran onstage for her first song bedecked in a phosphorescent ensemble by her favorite designer, Linda Gravenites. Joplin wore a royal-blue panne velvet vest lined with orchid-colored satin and trimmed with embroidery lifted from an Art Deco opera cloak. Underneath was a blouse of silk chiffon figured in velvet, shading from an iridescent silver to a deep loden shade, teamed with a pair of purple panne velvet trumpet-hemmed pants. Three months later, in its "Boutique" pages, *Vogue* ran a large picture of the singer flanked by a cross-section of her Garden audience. *Vogue* saluted "Janis Joplin the divine—when she shakes up the places like Madison Square Garden she's a flashing vision of violets and purples—of panne velvet, silvery chiffon . . . and Janis's audiences are helping to make purple hues big, too."

It was no longer unusual for *Vogue* and sister publications to acknowledge the fashion influence wielded by rock and popular musicians. During the '60s, their appeal had widened beyond the teenagers who had venerated them. With an estimated half of the American population under age twenty-one, popular music was hailed by some as the dominant expression of the age. Culture pundits turned an ensorcelled eye to contemporary music, as did fashion editors to the flamboyant looks used by star musicians to thumb their noses at the shibboleths of the mainstream. In the '60s, pop and rock stars were self-styled beauties who helped to ratify appreciation of the off beat that characterized the decade. "Unconventional-looking pop singers have done a lot to change the public concept of how people look," declared the owners of London's Ugly model agency in 1969. "Ten years ago, Ringo Starr would not have been admired at all."

In the late '60s, the rock hall replaced the discotheque as the prime arena for innovative fashion display. "In fashion terms a Fillmore East opening night deserves as much coverage as the Philharmonic Galanosed Galas," claimed the *Village Voice* shortly after the rock auditorium opened in March 1968. "It's a scene-making pageant whether they're seeing Lenny at Lincoln Center or Jimi at the Fillmore." In 1968, Bill Graham, the Fillmore's owner, tied together the pageantry in the audience with the fireworks on stage when he organized a mini-fashion happening during an interval in the evening's mixed bill. Unheralded, Barbara Mott, wife of designer Michael Mott, zoomed up the center aisle of the rock palace on an enormous Harley-Davidson. Dressed in Mott's black leather bra-top and miniskirt pegged with hobnail

Grace Slick performing with the Jefferson Airplane in the late '60s

Backstage at the Fillmore East

Barbara Mott astride her Harley-Davidson

studs, she tore up a ramp to the stage and parked her vehicle to the accompaniment of a cannonade of cheers from the Fillmore's audience.

The performers both mirrored the taste of their listeners and subtly warped or boldy advanced it. At the debut concert of the Velvet Underground in February 1966, it was appropriate that guitarist John Cale wear a rhinestone snake choker designed by Kenneth Jay Lane. The Underground was sponsored by Andy Warhol, and Lane had sparked a vogue for costume jewelry among the anciens and nouveaux riches who adopted Warhol and his entourage. For these women, Lane's faux animal bijouterie, patterned after similar fauna wrought in precious gems by jeweler David Webb, were identifiable trinkets. They were not as yet, however, common coin in the realm of men's attire, and thus did Cale invest Lane's gewgaw with a novel frisson.

One of the most influential fashion figures in London's rock galaxy was not a musician at all. Cathy McGowan, an Everywoman who had been picked to host the popular English music television show ''Ready, Steady, Go'' in 1963, swiftly became ''the mouthpiece for the great collective unconscious of British Pop," as Anthony Haden-Guest noted in 1967's *Birds of Britain*. McGowan wore the hottest design of the week by Biba, Foale and Tuffin, and other Mod cynosures as she introduced current groups performing their latest hits. "We used to sit and drool over her clothes," Twiggy recalled in her autobiography. "She was an idol to us because she was one of us." Distraught mothers wrote, imploring McGowan to wear the identical dress two weeks in succession so that their daughters would not bring the family to financial ruin. Disgruntled ready-to-wear manufacturers sent angry communiqués blaming her for business declines, "for when Cathy says something's out, it's out," *WWD*'s Ann Ryan noted in 1964. "Do you follow Paris?" McGowan was asked. "No. They copy us," she retorted. "One designer I know comes over regularly and pinches Mods' ideas."

The Beatles, the most popular pop group of the decade, had ridden the second wave of London's rejuvenation, "the great commercialization which began about in 1963," according to *Queen*'s Jocelyn Stevens. The clothes they donned smacked of Mod fashion, but were an arm's length away from the actual habiliments of young London trendies. Though their hair was long by American standards, it was styled like a boy's bowl cut; likewise, their collarless suits denoted a Peter Pan innocence. In *Getting It On: The Clothing of Rock 'N' Roll*, Mablen Jones writes that "their neat tailored clothes and polite manners were the answer to parental prayers for visual role models." In the U.S., where no tradition of Mod clothes existed, the insane success of their 1964 debut tour inspired endemic imitation by teenagers. But in the inner sanctums of London's "Modocracy" the Beatles in their early phases were considered cloying. "To be quite honest with you," one of the grapevine's voices recalls, "in those days the Beatles were regarded—fashion wise, particularly, and quite generally, amongst our sort of set if you like—as hicks. I mean they were these guys with silly suits and hairdos out from Liverpool of all places!" The Beatles were packaged to delight the adult world as much as its offspring, and Paris couturiers were among the captivated. In late 1965, it was reported that Courrèges had invited the Beatles to a Paris levée and promised in return he would design special raincoats for them to tote back to Britain's damp capital. The quartet was said to be more than willing, "but then premature leaks in a London paper queered the deal," *WWD* reported.

"If he gave nothing else to this world," rock critic Al Aronowitz eulogized, "Brian Jones was the first heterosexual male to start wearing costume jewelry from Saks Fifth Avenue." Writing soon after the death of the Rolling Stone's founder and rudder, Aronowitz recalled that the last time he had seen Jones, the musician was wearing a collar of day-glo sequins and a brace-

Guitarist John Hammond in snakeskin

Raunch onstage at the Fillmore East

let of watermelon seeds; Jones proudly vaunted the lavender suede boots he had recently acquired. He and his fellow Stones patterned themselves as unregenerate outlaws in direct contrast to the formula employed in the creation of the Beatles. Jones led the band to the farther shores of experimentation in clothes, steering them from their early black leather gear to the nether reaches of florid dandyism.

As Jones's companion, and later the common-law wife of Stones' guitarist Keith Richards, long, lean, blonde Anita Pallenberg was a tuning fork of fashion for the band and their retinue. "I was very kind of trendy in my own crazy way," she recalls. Pallenberg has survived many scandal-steeped years of drug addiction with Richards. Drug free, she now lives very quietly in London, attending a full-time program in fashion illustration at St. Martin's College of Art, thereby returning to her background in graphic design. Raised in Italy by German parents, as a child she designed her own clothes, made for her by the seamstress mother of a friend. For four years she studied graphic design in Munich and Rome, before a brief stint assisting a Roman couturière. Moving to New York in 1963, she became assistant to *Vogue* photographer Gianni Penati, occasionally sitting in for errant models, before returning to Europe, where she herself became a popular mannequin.

With the first money that I earned modeling I had to get some clothes, since I'd practically left America without anything. Instead of buying myself a nice proper outfit all I bought was a snakeskin jacket, and then later I had this kind of rat fur coat to go to work in. I found out that models are pretty kleptomaniacal. So I started to wear just the fur coat, with nothing underneath, so they wouldn't steal anything.

I used to do my shopping mostly at Les Puces. I always had a fascination for old clothes. I was going out every night to dance. I remember I found this transparent black dress, and I put just a black bikini underneath, and I went to Castel's like that, where there was this Italian prince. He sent me roses, saying it was "the first see-through dress" he'd ever seen.

Although she modeled the couture collections for European magazines, "I never really had a thing for *haute couture*," she says. I kind of looked down on it, really. Paris would come up with stuff that we'd been wearing for ages. I mean, I can live without being told what to wear." Pallenberg haunted the Chelsea Antique Market and stands around Europe, fascinated then as now by past cultures. Equally catalytic in her sartorial adventures was the "the acid, the drugs that we were putting inside ourselves. They gave you another outlook on things, a new feeling for color and materials."

A long power struggle between Jones and lead singer Mick Jagger culminated when Jones was dismissed from the band in June 1969. Soon afterward he drowned in his swimming pool. At a memorial concert the Stones presented in London's Hyde Park, Jagger unveiled a new, hermaphroditic persona that trumped the earlier heresies of Jones. He wore an elongated

(BELOW) Anita Pallenberg flanked by Mick Jagger and Keith Richards in 1968, soon after she completed filming Performance *with Jagger*

(BELOW, RIGHT) Brian Jones in 1967

jerkin, more a short dress than a long tunic, in white moiré over voile, and pipestem white pants. "The full, and unexpurgated story of how Rolling Stone Mick Jagger came to appear before a crowd of 250,000 wearing what one observer described as 'a little girl's white party frock,' can now be told to an expectant world," Christopher Ward announced in the *Daily Mirror*. The previous week, Jagger had searched for an outfit to a wear to an all-white dress ball given by Prince Rupert of Lowenstein. He found his ensemble at Michael Fish's Mayfair shop. For the Hyde Park performance, Jagger had bagged a snakeskin suit by London designer Ossie Clark, who turned out Jagger's wardrobe for his "Sympathy for the Devil" tour. The day of the Hyde Park concert dawned unexpectedly hot and sunny, however, and happenstance insured the tumult caused by Jagger's appearance that day in Hyde Park. His look has retained its androgynous flavor to the present day.

Mick Jagger at the July 1969 Rolling Stones concert in London's Hyde Park

When Mod was superseded by psychedelia in 1967, an anonymous London observer compared the two cultures: "the secret is everybody wears what they want to and there are no trend setters. The pop groups led Mod. The pop groups might be in this, but they're not the leaders." Yet the conversion of London's top groups to the mind-expanding fold, or its sartorial hallmarks, was inexorably persuasive. Vernon Lambert recalls the sensation aroused when the Who, formerly paragons of Mod, went on British television wearing bell-bottom trousers instead of stovepipes, and cotton sari shirts. The most dramatic and influential metamorphosis was effected by the Beatles. At the press party to launch the *Sergeant Pepper* LP, "the scrib-

Roger Daltry performing with The Who in 1969.

blers were kept manically busy describing the Famous Four's new line in threads,'' Derek Taylor, press representative for the band, recalls in *It Was Twenty Years Ago Today*.

Before marrying George Harrison, Pattie Boyd had been a popular London fashion model, and her tastes in fashion were closely monitored. Harrison raised eyebrows when she began patronizing The Fool, a federation of two Dutch designers, Marijke Koger and Joske Leeger, who were abetted by Koger's husband, Simjon, and associate Barry Finch. By appointment to the Beatle's court, The Fool poured moirés and satins into Hobbit shapes that were the ne plus ultra of psychedelic free association. "Where Did Pattie Get That Gear?" headlined a mesmerized Felicity Green in an August 1967 issue of the *Daily Mirror*. Green visited The Fool, reporting on their attire. Leeger wore "blue-printed, silk braid-bound pajamas, a blouse in three multi-coloured unrelated prints, snakeskin thong sandals up to her knees, a jeweled breast-

(LEFT) *Penny Beeching and Paulette Weider, guests at the wedding of Danny McCallock, bass guitarist of the Animals, in London, September 1967*

(RIGHT) *Betwixt and between Mod and psychedelia: Dusty Springfield and friend in London during the epochal summer of 1967*

plate, and a band and beads in her freak out hairdo so recently acclaimed by Paris." Marijke Koger was more sedately dressed in "pigtails, purple thong sandals, beads, a string of hippie bells and a multi-coloured minifrock in the psychedelic manner." Sporting "longer hair than either of the girls," Leeger's husband wore "a pendant, a purple velvet tunic, pale yellow peep-toe sandals, and some extremely form fitting pants in pink and lime satin stripes, bias cut."

Green's fascination was shared by many London aficionados, and in December of that year, the Beatles opened their Apple boutique, which stocked a comprehensive inventory of Fool designs. However, in a sudden decision, they closed the Baker Street shop the following July. The Fool had by this time decamped, following fallout from the local planning council over a cartoon-colored mural they had painted on Apple's exterior. Impulsively, the Beatles decided to give away the store's $36,000 stockpile of clothes and jewelry and bid adieu to the travails of shopkeeping.

The most electrifying women in popular music were the *jolie-laides*, the beautiful uglies, who refuted the homogenized prettiness of '50s songbirds. These reigning deities emboldened their audiences to exploit, rather than efface, their own idiosyncracies. Barbra Streisand epitomized the *jolie-laide* in the first half of the '60s. She refused to shorten her long Semitic nose, and saw her decision vindicated as her face became among the most photographed in the world. When Streisand was named to the world's best-dressed list, she boasted, "My nose helped put me on that list. . . . It's part of the look." Preparing for her first gigs in Manhattan *boîtes* at the turn of the '60s, Streisand combed through antique shops, fashioning a trademark mélange of '20s and '30s artifacts, which complemented her reconfiguring of musical chestnuts from these eras. As she ascended to the upper reaches of superstardom, however, her tastes became brassier. In January 1966, she was sent to Paris by Chemstrand, sponsor of her television specials, to shop the couture collections for an upcoming spectacular. The couture showings "all seemed flat until Barbra Streisand . . . showed up" *Time* reported. On her first trip abroad, twenty-four-year-old Streisand flouted custom by declining to wear a Chanel suit when she attended the legendary couturière's collection. Streisand swept into the salon wearing a jaguar-skin suit and Homberg "that had even the models gawking." Being true to herself meant not denying the bourgeois sensibilities of her upbringing in Brooklyn: "Those girls at Cardin's, they didn't have a thing under their dresses," she complained. "I was embarrassed." But in the late '60s, Streisand fell out of favor with hip youth as she spun her wheels in a succession of Hollywood extravaganzas. Her fashion identity became more diffused: at a benefit Courrèges fashion show held at "The Factory" in Los Angeles in November 1967 she

Barbra Streisand with Yves Saint Laurent backstage at Funny Girl *in 1965*

207

arrived "looking for all the world like one of the [Sunset] Strip's hippies," the *Times* reported. Yet the following spring, she accepted her Academy Award in a labored black chiffon peek-a-boo concoction crafted by custom dressmaker Arnold Scaasi.

Cass Eliot, alto lead of the Mamas and Papas, had been obese since childhood. Whatever personal torments her corpulence caused her, onstage her manner was sometimes lightly self-mocking, but not at all apologetic. The loose smock dresses and caftans of the '60s allowed her to dress fashionably and move with aplomb. "She throbbed and shimmied through a song," rock critic Richard Goldstein wrote, "jolting us into the realization that a fat girl could also be glamorous, if only she dared."

As a teenager, Janis Joplin was also a wallflower, unable to conform to the tenets of femininity as they were dictated in backwater Texas. She went instead to the opposite extreme, cultivating a blunt, "masculine" aggressiveness. Joplin's behavior further alienated her from her peers in the late '50s. A decade later, however, her blistering directness voiced contem-

The Mamas and the Papas in 1967

porary women's demand for an abolition of the double standard. "Don't you know you're nothing more than a one-night stand?" she taunted a paramour in a song lyric, silencing the gnawing doubt of earlier pop singers who pleaded: "Will you still love me tomorrow?"

"Janis was so damned magnetic! I was overwhelmed by her presence when I first met her," recalls Myra Friedman, Joplin's press representative and, later, biographer. "I got to thinking about the nature of her attractiveness, because she was not a pretty woman, in the customary way. I had to prepare something for the press, and I thought: 'She turns the definition of beauty counter clockwise.'" Joplin's skin was pimply, her features too sharp and large boned to cohere into chocolate-box comeliness. Yet her eyes were a captivating blue-gray, her face extraordinarily mobile, ignited by a restless animation and intelligence. Often, her face was puffy from dissipation, yet it also retained an unlikely innocence and incandescence. Joplin's personal magnetism enabled her to portray the beauty her hometown had insisted she could never possess. Her "metamorphosis from the ugly duckling of Port Arthur to the peacock of Haight-Ashbury meant," according to critic Ellen Willis, "that a woman who was not conventionally pretty . . . could not only invent her own beauty . . . but have that beauty appreciated."

In collaboration with a series of creative female mentors, Joplin coalesced a unique style that owed little, if anything, to establishment fashion. Joplin wanted to look "nifty at the very least, but preferably arresting and hopefully spectacular," says Linda Gravenites, who first saw Joplin perform soon after the singer moved to San Francisco in July 1966. She was then arrayed in a floor-length granny dress, a fad originated by Los Angeles teens in 1965. "I didn't think they suited at all. Janis was very feminine, but she wasn't, as I saw her, dainty in the least." A year later, Joplin asked Gravenites to make her an outfit for an upcoming concert. "I told her I saw her as a chick pirate wrapped in tawdry finery: laces and satins and bits and pieces from everywhere." The festive collage Joplin adopted was Haight-Ashbury's most eloquent sartorial imprimatur. In 1968, the twenty-five-year-old star issued a manifesto in defense of serendipity to the *Village Voice*. "Everybody's so hung up on the matching game—the shoes have to match the bag which matches the coat and dress. But the big question is, is it matching your soul? Your soul goes through changes, you're always feeling all things at once. So why not wear all things at once, its groovy—it's real." Joplin wore little make-up, which she dismissed as "a lot of insignificant crap." Rather than straighten her naturally crimpy hair, she heightened its kink by frizzing it outrageously. "Her look was not only different, it was logical—and practical. . . . She liberated more American women than a hundred books," rock critic Lillian Roxon wrote shortly after the singer's death.

In *Getting It On*, Mablen Jones describes the mythic stature embodied by Joplin and Grace Slick, lead singer of the Jefferson Airplane. They incarnated "Athena-like goddesses who were tough women." The war goddess's call to arms resounded through their unrepentant assault on all received codes of femininity. Unlike Joplin, however, Slick was unambiguously beautiful. She was endowed with velvety skin and lovely eyes: dark, luminous, piercing. She had done some modeling before joining the Airplane, and in 1967 her bangs were as glossy and tidy as a *Vogue* cover girl's, although later she opted for an exposed-wire hairstyle. Slick's cool self-possession made her the perfect foil to Joplin's white heat. While sometimes she opted for straightforward hip dress-up, Slick was at her most radiant in the quasi-mystical garb she adopted as the band first crested the psychedelia wave. In long flowing robes, she looked like a contemporary sibyl, a high priestess of acid to Joplin's neo-Dionysian maenad.

As Slick provided the perfect sounding board to Joplin, so soprano "Mama" Michelle Phil-

Janis Joplin and Tina Turner perform "Honky Tonk Woman" in 1969.

Sonny and Cher at a Hollywood film premiere in 1967

lips figured as a visual and vocal counterpoise to Cass Elliot. A sylph of the Hollywood canyons, Phillips's lissome blonde beauty embodied the California ideal celebrated in the surf anthems of the Beach Boys. Formerly a member of a folk combo directed by her husband, "Papa" John Phillips, she put a Los Angeles spin on the look of the folk madonnas of the early '60s, substituting jeans and western boots for their homespun skirts and tops. All four Mamas and Papas presented a united front of freewheeling West Coast eccentricity. "Aside from their talent," Dunhill Records' Jay Lasker said in 1967 of his decision to sign the group, "the biggest thing that impressed us was their appearance. They were so *odd.*" On their first album cover, the group was photographed entwined together in a rustic bathtub, and their reputation was secured. Their audiences responded, Michelle Phillips claimed, to "an image that was new, animated, and attractive and had women in it, liberated women yet." Yet despite the charisma of the female leads, it was John Phillips who was commissar of taste for the group. "However fancy our clothes, John forbade us to wear makeup or mess with our hair because it would be bad for our contemporary hippie image," Phillips writes in *California Dreamin'*. The quartet began to be outfitted by Antoinette Searles of Profils du Monde, a Beverly Hills atelier that, then as now, purveyed Eastern-inspired couture. In 1967, the Papas as well as the Mamas achieved their sartorial apotheosis draped in troubadour mantles made from brocades, damask, and matellase, chased with gold soutache, which glinted mysteriously like vestal offrey cloth.

Cher Bono was a dazzling *arbiter elegantiarum* in the Los Angeles musical firmament. Cher's Roman nose and shock of dark hair, the make-up that she adroitly applied in monochromatic relief, gave her a hybrid Mod and ethnic demeanor that was nonpareil in America

(LEFT) Tina Turner performing at Madison Square Garden in 1969, wearing a matte jersey dress by Dorothy Morgan

(RIGHT) Cher wearing a doeskin tunic in 1969

at the peak of Sonny and Cher's success in the mid '60s. "Jeered at by baffled adults, this bizarre song team—the latest in Pop music and Op fashion—are the soulmates of America's teenagers," Peter Bogdanovich reported in the *Saturday Evening Post* in 1966. Sonny, his dark hair worn in a neck-length pageboy, easily kept pace with his wife. To live the script of sartorial outlaw, rejection by the adult status quo was obligatory: Sonny and Cher could boast of being refused admission by the London Hilton and the Americana in New York. At a 1966 Hollywood Palladium benefit, Princess Margaret was in attendance, and Sonny and Cher's back-up musicians were dressed in the requisite black tie. Sonny, however, opted for a yellow turtleneck sweater and a white, double-breasted pirate's jacket with wide lapels, epaulettes, and yellow puffs for buttons. His tight, white trousers were embellished with a wide, silver-buckled, brown-leather belt and black boots. Cher sported a yellow-and-white striped suede cloth top, and white bell bottoms with yellow calvary stripes running down the sides. Backstage they were questioned by reporters about the recent dinner in Manhattan at which they had performed. A guest at the private repast was Diana Vreeland, who later became a mentor to the young pop heroine, commissioning Avedon to photograph her for several *Vogue* spreads. Cher boasted to the assembled scribes that at the dinner Jacqueline Kennedy had described Sonny's appearance as Shakesperean. "Did you wear a tuxedo *that* night?" Sonny was asked. "Nah," he shook his head. "I wore my bobcat vest. It would have been like what we usually wear is fraudulent if we dressed different that night."

Jimi Hendrix

"I'll have it!" Jimi Hendrix said to Vernon Lambert, while visiting his homestead at the Chelsea Antique Market in London. The roof of Lambert's stall was a concatenation of "heavily embroidered Spanish shawls, lace of Egyptian silver, antique saris, and marvelous passementerie from seventeenth-century curtains."

"Which, Jimi?" Lambert asked, only to find that Hendrix wanted the ceiling, lock, stock, and barrel; for the guitarist habitually enveloped his person and his environment in a cocoon of cloth overpowering in its plush sensuality.

En route to London in the fall of 1966, Hendrix abandoned the processed hair and natty suits of black rhythm-and-blues artists and met the British capital on its own terms, caparisoned full-throttle in a sartorial delirium triggered by the marriage of psychedelia and Mod. Hendrix managed to eclipse even Brian Jones, for he added the exotic attributes of black skin and an untamed Afro hairstyle, which sparked a rage for chemical frizzing among young white London blades. Hendrix's frilled, swagged, be-ribboned cloths of many colors suggested the vestments of a tribal shaman; his overtly sexual stage act legitimized peacock finery for young men in England and the U.S.

Colette Mimram, co-owner of a celebrated clothes shop on East Ninth Street in Manhattan, decorated Hendrix's Greenwich Village abode with nomadic pillows, tie-dyes, and African materials from the Village boutique Knobkerry. She remembers Hendrix visiting her once in Morocco, causing a sensation when he stepped off the plane in an astounding outfit consisting of fringed shawl, vest, jacket, and pants. Toward the end of his life, however, Hendrix was toning down into an earthier register. "He was becoming a little subdued towards the end, with the naturals and the beiges," Mimram recalls. "But even if it was all beige, he'd like to have a very bright Indian silk scarf tied around. It looked *great* on him. He *loved* those colors!"

The rock stars sought to stay one step ahead of their fans and most vehemently, their imitators in the "straight" world. As the 1960s unfolded, however, the threshold of *épater* in dress was inexorably rising. "There's no sense trying to shock people with the way you dress," Cher cautioned in 1968. "They don't shock easily any more." Like Jimi Hendrix, Janis Joplin was experimenting with a less inflammatory look at the very end of her life. In the days before her death, she had dieted, methodically acquired a sun tan, and gone to a Los Angeles hairdresser to have her hair streaked. Would she eventually return to her conservative roots, if only once more to proclaim her status as trend setter? Myra Friedman recalls walking with Joplin in 1970 past Paraphernalia at 55th Street and Lexington Avenue. The window was chock full of hip clothes, the very torches she had once set to the deadwood of Seventh Avenue. "Janis looked at the window," Friedman recounts, "turned to me and rolled her eyes. Laughing, she railed: 'Next I'll have to start wearing tweed suits!'"

SWAN SONG

One is tempted to call the years 1967 to 1970 unique in the recorded history of dress and adornment. Fashion splintered into countless modules, ranging from costume montages to minimalist body coverings to purely conceptual garment projections. "Fashion is experiencing one of the most interesting dilemmas in its history," Brigid Keenan wrote in Britain's *Nova* in 1968. "There is a state of anarchy." A toppling of fashion's pyramidal stratification seemed to have occurred, a rerouting of the dissemination process. Fashion's leaders were now, as Betsey Johnson tallied in February 1969, "the kids who put it all together themselves." Neither the couture nor Seventh Avenue could compete in news value and substantive impact with the prismatic combinations of handcraft and folk costume invented by youth. Their dress revealed an infinity of unique permutations.

Sifting through contemporary press, one is amazed at how contagious were the battle cries of youth. By obeying the spirit, rather than the letter, of the subculture's looks and life-style, people of many ages realized that they could unfetter themselves. In July 1968, *WWD* issued a carillon of guarded support: "The Kooks, the Kids, and the Hippies got people to start thinking in a fresh way. You may not agree with them, but you can't ignore them. They freed themselves . . . and gave others the courage to do the same." In place of the wonted reign of chic, a new imperative of raised consciousness ruled the fashionables. It was démodé not to, at the least, pay lip service to youth's manifestos of personal authenticity and self-expression; it was passé to dress in the ossified uniforms of the rich. Liberality in dress connoted a flexible mind able to understand, if not participate in challenges to men's and women's respective positions, to society's pecking orders and governmental policy. The eclectic potpourris of the late 1960s became a sign of the individual's dissent from the corporate state. Subjective preference rather than obedience to ordained norms was trumpeted as the true criterion of fashionability. When *1969: The Year in Review* looked back at the year's fashions, it saw they "had nothing to do with any particular hemline or cut of cloth. The main thing was feeling. The idea was that if you wore what felt good, at any particular time or place, you were in fashion."

It became an article of faith among the hip fashion-conscious that one's dress was meant to illustrate the authentic self and psyche. "Finding a look," *WWD* noted in 1968, "is almost like going through analysis. . . . To find a personal expression of beauty, one has to search the soul." With identities of institutions and individual in flux, however, and with so wide a diapason from which to choose, the individual remade himself daily, trying out new stances of dress and behavior, internalizing some, keeping others at arm's length as theatrical alter egos. "Today nothing is out because everything is in. Every costume from every era is now available

"Overnight, fashion has turned from a humorless cult, ruled by a few high priests, into a game that anybody can play, any way they want to play it," William Zinsser editorialized in Life *in May 1968. Shown here, part of the follies: poster dresses fabricated in 1968 by Harry Gordon, an American graphic artist.*

Jean Shrimpton being styled for a 1969 Vogue shoot in London, wearing a patchwork panne velvet dress designed by Laura Jessop for The Sweet Shop on King's Road

to everyone. 'Nowadays the doorman doesn't know who to let in,'" Marshall McLuhan registered in 1968.

Communities that spawned these beliefs became the fountainheads of fashion. Hairdresser Paul McGregor explained his move from Manhattan's East Midtown down to St. Mark's Place in the East Village: "Uptown is so corny. . . . It's here where things are happening." "So many of the New York stores try to be 'with it,' but they don't know anything about the Electric Circus or Salvation," Halston, then director of custom millinery at Bergdorf Goodman, complained in 1968. "They don't show up at the boutiques in the Village or Madison Avenue. . . . They don't ever listen to the new music. It's a full-time job just to be aware of what's going on."

Fashion looked for novel forums in which these adventurous new ideas could be tested, exchanged, ricocheted between participants. A mellowing of cold, cruel Manhattan was heralded by the heterogenous yet harmonious crowds clustering around Central Park's Bethesda Fountain, now a stage for fashion of every genre. The clothes worn there were so spectacular that in 1968 WWD devoted two double-page spreads to the panoply swirling around the esplanade. "From a place where no one would be caught ever," the park was now "the grooviest social happening on any good weather weekend. A comment overheard seemed to sum up the new feeling about the park: 'It's more fun here than out at my house in Fire Island.'" The action at Bethesda Fountain provided "proof that there is no one look . . . individuality is what scores." WWD saw "get-ups that range from Indian to Emily Brontë . . . and a few for which there is no name."

"Never were people more creative about dressing than at that time," declares Frances Patiky Stein. The fascination with Middle and Far Eastern dress guaranteed tremendous latitude by the very nature of draped clothing. "I remember so well a dinner at my house, at which Loulou de la Falaise, Marisa and Berry Berenson each wore a remarkable turban tied together with Byzantine intricacy out of at least four pieces of thinnest Indian bias-cut fabric. Each one was different and each tied a turban better than the other. I remember standing over them, trying to understand how each of them did it," recalls Stein. Similarly, the traditional African and East Indian crafts of batik and tie-dying were everywhere in the late '60s, spraying a mottled, light-dappled wash that could never stamp two garments identically.

The tactility of fabric clued in to the heightened sensitivity engendered by the LSD experience and the hedonistic euphoria resulting from a breakdown of sexual taboos. "Feel-good" clothes dominated every stratum of fashion during these last years of the decade. Velvet reigned as the epoch's quintessential cloth, ubiquitous in a sensual variety of weaves and

Londoners Gillian Williams and Dean Horrigan share a Lurex Siamese-twin jumpsuit from Henry Moss in 1969.

wefts: crushed into a veined network of creases, incised into cut velvet's two-dimensional, high pile/low pile bas relief. Slithery charmeuse and gently caressing matte jersey were also paradigmatic coverings for the footloose bodies of the late '60s. Satin, damask, brocade, watered silk, nappy crêpe—these stuffs entranced the eye and invited the touch and so became iconic.

As society would be overhauled, so would the bedrock elements of clothing. The dress was an anachronism, Rudi Gernreich and others prognosticated—it would become an accessory rather than the cornerstone of a woman's wardrobe. "I believe the body stocking or a form of it will be the main element of fashions of the future," forecasted Jacques Fontery, who had made space suits of obscure synthetics and mesh for the film *Barbarella*. Some designers anticipated that technological advances would foster an unprecedented vocabulary of clothing. Paco Rabanne predicted in 1966 that within five years women's clothes would be "glued on, what we call 'collant' in French." Mary Quant hypothesized in 1967 that "Some day we will blow clothes the way people blow glass. It's ridiculous that fabric should be cut up to make a flat thing to go round a round person."

The interstice of art object and garment blurred as art cut loose from the confines of the wall-hung object and fashion evolved into ambulatory membranes. In September 1967, Diana Dew, a pioneer proponent of the dress as kinetic art, left Paraphernalia to pursue environmental design free from the constrictions of wholesale manufacturing. Howard Smith reported in the *Village Voice* that Dew, "who likes to think about clothes more as sculpture," thought that art collectors would be her ideal audience, since she believed "a dress, when not on the back, should hang on the wall and be plugged in." Experiments like Dew's began to make clothing an appropriate subject for museum exposure. In 1967, the Metropolitan Museum's *Art and Fashion* exhibit devoted a gallery to contemporary fashions in which Rabanne's chain-mail doublets and Dew's electrical light-up dresses were installed. In 1968, New York's Museum of Contemporary Crafts' *Body Covering* show unveiled speculative new body containers, the temperature of which would respond to fluctuations in the surrounding environment. An article of clothing might, in theory, shelter a community rather than only an individual. James Lee Byars unfurled epic-sized tentlike cocoons in silk, collectively inhabited by human flotillas. They trotted across the streets of Manhattan, only their heads visible, enveloped in this ideologically weighted variant of performance and site-specific art.

The resurrection of antique garments was the ultimate victory of the iconoclast over the fashion politburo. For while the fashion industry could produce period homages and historical pastiches, it could not, by definition, retail secondhand garments. By-passing department stores and designer showrooms, the votaries of this movement flocked instead to the world's

Maning sketch of model Pat Cleveland in futuristic "second skins" from Santos Santiago

André Murasan painted the clothes, the decor, and the furnishings in his Greenwich Village shop.

souks, antique stalls, and open-air bazaars, discovering a cornucopia of still affordable booty from bygone eras.

Fashion changed so rapidly during the '60s that by the end of the decade the hottest trends of the mid '60s could be viewed as if in aspic. Beached by shifting tides, or by their own peccadillos, many of the leading lights of Pop New York had now been deposed. One of the first to fall to earth was Tiger Morse, who at the end of the decade was reduced to waiting tables at Max's Kansas City.

"It's a cross-section of decadence, isn't it?" a titillated spectator had asked at one of Morse's blast-offs. Morse cultivated her mien of debauchery to the designer's profit and the

amusement of her audience, but her dissipation was not a pose. Morse was immersed in the city's amphetamine subculture. One top designer of the decade tells a sad story: "An editor was describing to me how when you were sent clothes from a designer's showroom you were usually sent the clothes neatly wrapped—period. When Tiger sent something over, you got the dress as well as the misplaced cotton ball or syringe cap." In 1967, she had agreed to open a retail boutique at the Salvation discotheque. Morse stayed on the premises, but the boutique did not fly—for three months she locked herself into the raw space she was supposed to be constructing. In the spring of 1970, Morse announced she was liquidating the contents of her loft to raise money. She was retaining her capacious archive of antique clothing, as well

Thea Porter, London's sultana of Near Eastern fashion, presented this aluminum cloth djellaba in 1968.

as a haul of silk-screen vinyl dresses and her prototype white sequin electric dress; they were now period pieces. Six months before she died, Morse claimed to a friend to be totally detoxed, but in 1972 she died of an overdose of sleeping pills.

It was inevitable that contemporary fashion's voracious foraging for ethnic veracity would lead it to the veldts and forests of the African continent. But, more significantly, the adoption of autochthonous African costume signified the racial pride inculcated by the Civil Rights movement. The black middle class had long shied away from visual identification with their forebears. Making it in American society meant dressing to facilitate assimilation. Blacks had been systematically educated in self-hatred, indoctrinated to respect only Caucasian norms of appearance and dress. "I learned a big lesson from a star who'd just arrived in Hollywood in the '50s," recalls L.A. designer Bob Rogers, who costumed Dionne Warwick in full African pageantry for the 1969 film *Slaves*. "I went to his house with some beautiful shirts made out of Mexican cotton." Though Rogers had been introduced to the young performer "by a well-known painter who was this star's mentor in terms of taste," the actor demurred. "He'd worn that kind of fabric—he called it sackcloth—as a kid and he was trying to get away from that. He wanted nothing but soft, smooth things against his skin. The black middle class is not going to wear any rough material like that, baby, when they know that silk is the thing!"

As always, Paris was erotically intoxicated with the noble savagery of African culture. For

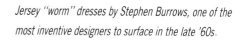

Jersey "worm" dresses by Stephen Burrows, one of the most inventive designers to surface in the late '60s.

The Voices of East Harlem perform in the late '60s.

Naomi Sims in Stephen Burrows's brown panne velvet pants, suede sporran, and cowhide bolero, photographed on Fire Island in 1968

Courrèges's 1968 couture showings, the designer recruited Leon Hillard of the Harlem Globetrotters to pepper the proceedings. Dressed in a striped and star-spangled red, white, and blue Uncle Sam outfit, Hillard twirled a basketball with nimble prowess, as Courrèges's models made their characteristically staccato, unpredictably timed entrances.

The late '60s also saw the least empowered population in fashion—women themselves—organize a concerted, implacable demand for equality. Although in the 1970s the women's movement would reinterpret the miniskirt as an instrument of exploitation, the fashion for shorter skirts was perceived as a yardstick of liberation during the garment's actual vogue. In 1968, James Laver called it "the final word in the emancipation of woman—in proving her economic independence. Long, hampering skirts were fetters to keep a woman at home." The

Elena Solow with Dr. Benjamin Spock

return of calf-length skirts, which began to be promoted by the fashion industry around 1967, was received as an unmistakably reactionary assault. Reviewing Gernreich's knitwear collection in May 1968, Bernadine Morris wrote approvingly in the *New York Times* that the group "affirmed his belief that modern women are bold and strong—not fainting violets." Gernreich eschewed calf-grazing, petticoat buttressed skirts, wasp waistlines, "and the trappings that other designers have held out to lull women into a false sense of nineteenth century protectedness."

Throughout the '60s, dress telegraphed a gulf between factions that were in the know, and those who clung to the values of the past. Yet battlelines between the progressive and old

Jane Fonda in a poncho from the unnamed boutique at
321 East 9th Street in Manhattan

guard began to blur late in the decade. Fashion is a potent transmitter of changes in sensibility; it was difficult for the bourgeois to appropriate fashions of disenfranchised cultures without an acknowledgment of their provenance. Likewise, the couture was palpably reluctant to legitimize the incursions of youth. But by the late '60s, no couturier was ignoring the phantasmagorical licence introduced on San Francisco's Haight Street or London's King's Road. Even the aristocratic Mme. Grès, *Vogue* observed, was "having a bit of fun with the Indians." Translating gypsy, ethnic, and hippie motifs into the world's most sumptuous fabrics produced ravishing, if slightly stilted visions. For Ungaro's July 1969 showings, Sonia Knapp outlined enormous colored sun goggles around the models's eyes, from which radiated dots, tear drops,

Janis Joplin arriving at the Woodstock Festival in August 1969, wearing tie-dye separates from The Fur Balloon boutique of New York

and vectors in contrasting tones. Previewing his January 1970 collection, Ungaro confided that Knapp's prints now would be hallucinogic: "dream-like. Not vivid prints but colors which almost escape color. Colors which blend together. . . . I almost wish they will not be able to remember the colors." Primary shades were Givenchy's handle on a gypsy look. "*My* gypsy," he emphasized. "The well dressed Bohemian. The luxurious gypsy."

The couture fabricated a realm of pure style devoid of ideology. The duchess of Windsor in Saint Laurent's patchwork skirt evoked late eighteenth-century nobles blithely posing in the garb of a shepherdess. In the '60s, as in the rococo, the gilded toyed with the picturesque manners of the less fortunate. Inevitably, the ideological freight of the counterculture's sar-

228

Bizet's Carmen *was one of the most provocative archetypes revived during the late '60s.*

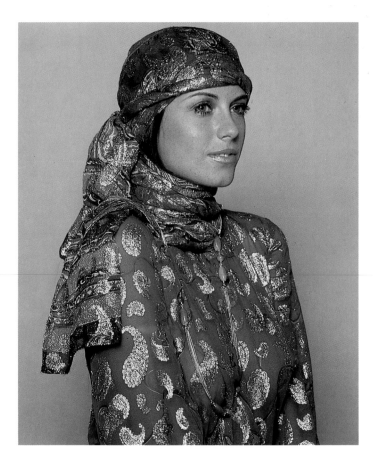

Chiffon evening dress from Marc Bohan's fall 1969 couture collection for the House of Dior

torial keynotes became muted as they were co-opted. Some merchants, however, were determined that the symbols would not be denatured. When Sara Penn, owner of the boutique Knobkerry, arrived in New York in the early 1950s, she spent nights in west Greenwich Village drinking the first cups of espresso sold in the city. By 1965, when she opened her store, the hub of bohemia was shifting east. Once called the Lower East Side, New York's downtown Eastern European ghetto was fast being renamed the East Village. An avant-garde colony took root when artists began fleeing the spiraling rents and raucous crowds that had descended upon the West Village during the folk music craze of the early '60s. "I'd been a social worker at Mobilization for Youth on the Lower East Side, working with drug-abusing teenage gangs," Penn explains. "I decided that I didn't want to continue." Penn's store supplied a personal demand echoed by women across the city. "I wanted to wear pants. I wanted all kinds of pants

Joan Buck in Ossie Clark's crêpe printed with a Celia Birtwell design

Alice Pollack, Ossie Clark, and Chelita Secunda (partially hidden) at a party they threw at London's Royal Albert Hall to welcome New Year, 1969

Stephen Burrows's stitched leather pants worn with a '40s blouse

Sant' Angelo's signature look blended far-reaching folklore influences.

to be accessible." Knobkerry began as a source for softly draped Indian chari-door, guerrara, and chalwal pantaloons.

The integrity of the civil rights crusader could, in the '60s, dovetail very easily with the intransigence of a champion of avant-garde regalia. "At Settlement for Youth we wanted to dramatize a little fable by George Bernard Shaw called 'The Adventures of a Black Girl in her Search for God.'" Shaw's parable extolls a child in South Africa who "leaves a mission, takes off all her clothes, and just goes out with a knobkerry. Anytime she encounters anyone who tries to tell her who God is, she just hits them with this stick and keeps going in her personal search." Shifting from social work to retail, Penn retained the "Knobkerry" as a personal symbol. "I thought, if anybody tells us what fashion is, we're just going to hit them with our 'stick'—our store. We'll discover our own fashion."

Called by *New York* magazine "Sara Penn's big/little star shop" on account of the celebrities who came to patronize it, Knobkerry was a clearing house for reciprocal translations between Western and exotic fabrics and shapes. It also offered unique pieces of African body adornment and handicraft. For Penn, Knobkerry was "a political statement to get people to know these countries," recalls Elena Solow, who worked part time in the store while she coordinated antiwar activist pediatrician Dr. Benjamin Spock's speaking engagements. "Whenever we sold something we explained where it was from, about the people and their philosophies, all the history that we were never taught growing up in the U.S. Sara kept all these books and maps and we had to teach ourselves about places we'd never heard of. I remember trying to tell Jimi Hendrix's drummer once about where this tenting he wanted came from. I don't think he was real interested. But some people were."

Penn's store became a crown jewel in the extraordinary *parure* carved out on Saint Mark's Place, the main shopping artery traversing the hippie community of the East Village. During the late '60s, recalls Pilar Crespi, Saint Mark's Place "was unlike any other street in the world." When the homesteading beatniks of the early '60s were augmented by intrepid hippies, the East Village mushroomed into a counterculture sideshow. During its halcyon days, the area was anchored by the Fillmore East at Second Avenue and 5th Street, and the Electric Circus, three blocks to the north. People from all over the city flocked to see the district's indigenous fashions, many spawned at the tiny stores that sprung up like goldenrod on Saint Mark's Place and adjacent blocks. In the East Village, the philosophical tenets of the retail store were brought into accordance with the tribal ethic of the drop-out culture. The pillaging capitalism of Tiger Morse was now unacceptable. "We hated the idea of a boutique," Colette Mimram and Stella Douglas told Blair Sabol of the *Village Voice* when they opened their store

Peasant separates by Ingeborg Marcus

236

Mr. and Mrs. Michael Mott denaturing military costume at an antiwar protest outside the Pentagon in Washington, D.C.

at 321 East 9th Street in the fall of 1968. "What we strived for was almost a trading post where we could sell what we've scored on our trips to Morocco and Europe." Mimram and Douglas insisted on the latitude necessary if commerce were not to cramp an individual's lifestyle. They wanted "plenty of freedom so we can keep strange store hours . . . that *WE* feel like keeping." They intended their store to blossom into a community crafts clubhouse. "We're a workshop, not a factory," Douglas told Sabol. "We create, not reproduce."

"I was very Gucci/Pucci," recalls Colette Mimram. Twenty-two at the time, Mimram had been raised in Morocco by French parents and worked in New York as a photographic stylist. One day in the early autumn of 1968, Mimram and Douglas had gone shopping together in Greenwich Village. They happened upon a shop entitled Wisdom and Folly, on East 9th Street, where their senses were arrested by the pungent aroma of marijuana as well as an extraordinary pair of straight-leg beige leather pants, edged with white American Indian fringes, which glistened with glass and ceramic beads sewn at the bottom of each strip. "God, I'd love to have a pair of pants like that," Mimram recalls thinking. "I just felt like doing something crazy. I didn't think that I could actually wear them—it was like a costume. I never thought that they could be an everyday pair of pants for me—but that's how they ended up."

Three young artisans—Timothy DeWitt, Lee Zontone, and Kyle Banks—ran the store and produced custom-made leather haberdashery. They told Mimram and Douglas that they were about to be evicted. Mimram returned to order a fringed jacket to go with the pants and to propose that they combine forces. "They said there was a location across the street, but they couldn't afford to take it." The two women proposed renting the store themselves and providing the basement as a workroom. "They told us that they would love to, although they probably wondered: 'Who are those two uptown chicks?' with an accent no less." For two crowded years the never-named boutique at 321 East 9th Street was one of New York's most unusual cloth-

ing stands. "I lost my tunnel vision, and I realized that there was much more than just Madison Avenue," Mimram says. "It was a great awakening for me."

"It was that desire to change things around completely: the look, the world!" Such was the impulse to which Chelita Secunda ascribes her decision, in the mid '60s, to dye her hair electric blue and slather glitter over her person. Secunda was muse to Ossie Clark, who, with Alice Pollack, founded "Quorum," a boutique/wholesale enterprise located just off King's Road. Quorum was a hive of activity; sandwiched between the ground-floor retail space and the workrooms at the top of the building were the modeling agency English Boy as well as a hideaway used by Rolling Stone Brian Jones. Quorum was a magnet for London's *haute bohême*; it galvanized the city's free spirits of means. "We were against marriage, against war," says Secunda, who managed Quorum from 1966 to 1969. "We believed love could change everything, that one's freedom to say, do, dress as you wanted was a birthright. Nobody had a right to tell you otherwise. If you wanted to wear this and this together, it was all right, whereas that hadn't happened before." Earlier in the decade, Secunda had been fired by an editor of *Harper's Bazaar* for the transgression of wearing shades of blue and green together to work. "One had always conformed to certain rules," she says. "Suddenly they were thrown out the window."

Quorum was famous for perfectly cut trouser suits in printed velvets and satins; Clark's bias-cut crêpe and chiffon hugged the body before flowing into billowy handkerchief points. Clark, a graduate of the Royal College, used remarkable textiles by his wife, Celia Birtwell, who was influenced by Leon Bakst's stylization of Grecian flora and fauna in his decor and costumes for the Ballets Russes. Bakst's sylvan imagery once again surfaced when Sotheby's auctioned a fabulous trove of vintage ballet costumes in 1967.

Although England's economic boom was now slackening, London was still in overdrive, the city of milk and honey to dreamers around the world. London's *joie de vivre* bubbled from Quorum, which staged lavish fashion shows at large venues throughout the city. Secunda recalls a particularly festive gala at the Chelsea Town Hall. "All the press and buyers were in the main hall, and then there was a room at the back, for all the friends: the Beatles (Pattie Harrison was modeling for us), the Stones, Hockney—cheering and carrying on. It was all very incestuous."

"She patters along through Notting Hill Gate in her printed chiffons," was how *WWD*'s Jo-An Jenkin's sighted Zandra Rhodes in August 1969: "head swathed in turbans and a dozen five and dime store rings on her fingers, her eyes batting scarlet lashes, and shadowed blue and yellow. Heads swivel as she goes—but Zandra doesn't care." Rhodes's personal appearance has never been limited by known prototypes; as a fashion designer, she is also an auto-didact, having graduated from the Royal College of Art with a degree in textile rather than fashion design. After graduating in 1964, Rhodes endured several years of mixed success and vicissitudes before seeing her talent flower gloriously at the end of the decade. "I don't feel I totally fit into a category, but I was lucky to come along at the culmination of the '60s. It was like a loophole, where people could accept what I did." Rhodes attributes her perseverance to "a very strong mother who gave confidence." Beatrice Rhodes, who died in 1968, was a fashion instructor at the Medway College of Art. Her appearance was also flamboyant: "She looked

As the counterculture began to deflate, the couture began a pitched attack against the forces of insurrection. In July 1969, Saint Laurent had included a heavy dosage of calf-length skirts—termed the "midi" by *WWD*—as part of a varied continuum of lengths seen in his collection. His long skirts were originally seen as a gesture of deference to youth, whose affinity for peasant and antique styles had already led them for several seasons to experiment with longer skirts. Ernestine Carter, fashion matriarch of the London *Sunday Times*, commented after Saint Laurent raised the curtain in July 1969: "He's given direction and authority to the London Kinks. All those granny dresses and things we've seen in Chelsea for a couple of years." Six months later, however, the economic retrenchment that began to take root was curtailing the spending of American women; store buyers were "praying for the kind of fashion news that will demand complete new wardrobes," *WWD* reported. Wholesale fabric manufacturers, too, were eager to see skirts lengthen. An anonymous fiber producer told *WWD*: "Changing the hemline isn't like throwing a pebble into a pool, it's like tossing in a washing machine."

Paris issued a party line in January 1970: only Ungaro's and Courrèges's skirts remained higher than calf length. "By next fall the short skirt will be démodé," Sidney Gittler of Ohrbach's crowed. "The women are going to fight like hell, but they are going to set a match to their wardrobes." The relief of many in the press was palpable, too. *WWD*'s June Weir expressed her pleasure that there was "nothing hippie, tuned-in, turned-on or freaky" about Paris's new directives. Between the stitches, the long skirt contained a trenchant subtext of sexual, social, and political reaction. Givenchy promised his midis would "make women react in a more feminine way." Saint Laurent issued an execution order to the reign of grass-roots influence. "Finished are the hippie things . . . all those bits of folkore . . . those scarves. The street is terrifying now, horrible." In March 1970, Gloria Steinem wrote in *New York*: "It is as if the Silent Majorities of France and America got fed up with styles dictated by what were, according to both *haute couture* and suburban standards, the outcast groups. . . . Manufacturers are hurrying back to styles set by the affluent, the perpetrators of Conventional Wisdom."

Given the cyclical operation of fashion, it was inevitable that skirts would lengthen—but the late '60s were not a time of business as usual. Had fashion been allowed to evolve organically, it would surely have done so within a context of eclecticism. The midi juggernaut flew in the face of contemporary events: for the women's movement was now proliferating throughout America. The industry's *putsch* did not take into account women's new militancy. "It almost seems as if the buyers and designers are testing out the supreme vulnerability of the female consumer," Blair Sabol analyzed. "They want to see how heavy a power trip they can maintain by pushing a design that completely contradicts our way of living."

Fashion continued on its anarchic course throughout 1970. Visiting New York that year, Zandra Rhodes saw "an explosion of ideas . . . a new freedom in thinking and an acceptance of individuality." The catholic tastes of the late '60s were for a time bolstered by the plethora of different lengths. "It was a glorious moment in fashion history," Kitty Kelly recalled two years later in *The Wonderful World of Women's Wear Daily*, "perhaps the one moment afforded a woman whereby she could be totally and completely independent."

The fashion establishment became more and more aggressive about protecting its investment and imposing its will, but the midi blitz turned into a full-scale fiasco. In the first half of 1971, *Vogue* and *Harper's Bazaar* lost a third of their advertising pages. Both magazines consequently underwent personnel shakedowns. The recession that shook the country's general economy was exacerbated by the crisis rending fashion; an even greater panic and conservatism riddled the industry. In July 1971, Grace Mirabella replaced Diana Vreeland as Editor-in-Chief of *Vogue*. The magazine no longer paid lip service to ecumenism but instead announced mulishly: "Don't be confused. This is the Look." During the first years of the '70s, the glossies proclaimed joyously that normalcy had returned, that the delirium of the recent past was now vanquished. A slew of inoffensively all-American fashion models reigned, women who "with a tactical makeup change could be asking you to fly them to Miami," as Owen Edwards wrote in *New York* in 1973. *Vogue* urged its readers to be grateful for the new mood of retrenchment. Concurrent with the backlash in high fashion, however, the women's movement began to preach categorical disdain for the institution of fashion. It encouraged women to dress casually in pants and shirts—as had members of left wing movements in the '60s—and concentrate their energies on systematically reshaping their lives.

The anything-goes euphoria of the last years of the '60s had receded into legend by 1973. "The climate is particularly uncongenial to rebels at the moment," Kennedy Fraser divined that year. Fraser noted that many of the rights won in the '60s "have been judiciously purged. The fashion industry—both male and female divisions—in brushing aside the charades and cultivated childishness of style set out to reestablish confidence in the familiar, grown-up rules." During the early '70s, "Innovators and nonconformists were firmly pushed out in the cold."

The last twenty years have brought women into positions of power, the attainment of which would have been a pipe dream during the early '60s. Yet, while the women's movement had earlier advocated a reform of the social and political superstructure, some of its later manifestations were of "a narrow feminism that advocated women's advancement within the existing society," as Helen Lefkowitz Horowitz writes in *Campus Life*. As women availed themselves of unprecedented opportunities in business, they bought into the conformist belief systems of the corporate world, with a concomitant loss of liberty and self-expression in dress. Benedetta Barzini theorizes that "the *espace* given by the thought of freedom creates anxiety. So the reaction to a big declaration of freedom is today's restriction: You must be properly dressed if you want to get into business. People believe that they must look right to get ahead, and their belief is self-fulfilling. It's always been true, but today it's the dominant idea. The '60s were a cry of innovation and freedom. The response to that was fear and closure."

While the envisioned utopia did not materialize, the legacy of the '60s has proved enduring. Unconstructed clothes continued to dominate fashion through the late '70s, while pants for women are today a commonplace. The relaxation of dress codes wrought by the '60s now seems nearly irrevocable. During the 1980s, Establishment fashion began turning to the right; in response, youth gravitated to the '60s as a reference point of rebellion, celebrating its breakthroughs and recycling its decorative motifs. The dialectic of fashion continues.

BIBLIOGRAPHY

Adams, Hugh. *Art of the Sixties.* London: Peerage Books, 1978.

Aitken, Jonathan. *The Young Meteors.* New York: Athenaeum, 1967.

Alloway, Lawrence. *American Pop Art.* New York: Whitney Museum of American Art, 1978.

Anthony, Gene. *The Summer of Love, A Photo-Documentary.* Berkeley: Celestial Arts, 1980.

Bailey, David, and Peter Evans. *Goodbye Baby and Amen: A Sarabande for the Sixties.* New York: Coward-McCann, 1969.

Balfour, Victoria. *Rock Wives.* New York: Beech Tree Books, 1986.

Banner, Lois W. *American Beauty.* New York: Alfred A. Knopf, 1983.

Barwick, Sandra. *A Century of Style.* London: George Allen & Unwin, 1984.

Batterberry, Michael and Ariane. *Fashion/The Mirror of History.* New York: Greenwich House, 1977.

Bell, Quentin. *On Human Finery.* New York: Schocken Books, 1976.

Bender, Marilyn. *The Beautiful People.* New York: Coward-McCann, 1967.

Berch, Bettina. *Radical by Design: The Life and Style of Elizabeth Hawes, Fashion Designer, Union Organizer, Best-Selling Author.* New York: E. P. Dutton, 1988.

Bockris, Victor, and Gerard Malanga. *Uptight: The Velvet Underground Story.* New York: Quill, 1985.

Bond, David. *The Guinness Guide to 20th-Century Fashion.* London: Guinness Superlatives Ltd., 1981.

Brady, James. *Superchic.* Boston: Little, Brown, 1974.

Brain, Robert. *The Decorated Body.* New York: Harper & Row, 1979.

Brown, Peter, and Steven Gaines. *The Love You Make.* New York: McGraw-Hill Book Company, 1983.

Callan, Michael Feeny. *Julie Christie.* New York: St. Martin's Press, 1984.

Carter, Ernestine. *The Changing World of Fashion.* New York: G. P. Putnam's Sons, 1977.

Castle, Charles. *Model Girl.* Secaucus, New Jersey: Chartwell Books, Inc., 1977.

Chafe, William Henry. *The American Woman: Her Changing Social, Economic, Political Roles, 1920–1970.* New York: Oxford University Press, 1972.

Coleridge, Nicholas. *The Fashion Conspiracy.* New York: Harper & Row, 1988.

Core, Philip. *The Original Eye: Arbiters of Twentieth Century Taste.* London, Melbourne, New York: Quartet Books, 1984.

Daves, Jessica. *Ready-Made Miracle.* New York: G. P. Putnam's Sons, 1967.

Devlin, Polly. *Vogue Book of Fashion Photography.* New York: Simon and Schuster, 1979.

Dickstein, Morris. *Gates of Eden.* New York: Basic Books, 1977.

Dorfles, Gillo. *Kitsch: The World of Bad Taste.* New York: Universe Books, 1979.

Drake, Nicholas. *The Sixties: A Decade in Vogue.* Englewood Cliffs, New Jersey: Prentice-Hall, 1988.

Edelstein, Andrew J. *The Pop Sixties.* New York: World Almanac Publications, 1985.

Evans, Sara. *Personal Politics: The Roots of Women's Liberation in the Civil Rights Movement and the New Left.* New York: Alfred A. Knopf, 1979.

Fairchild, John. *The Fashionable Savages.* New York: Doubleday, 1965.

Finkelstein, Nat. *Andy Warhol: The Factory Years, 1964–1967.* New York: St. Martin's Press, 1989.

Fraser, Kennedy. *The Fashionable Mind.* New York: Alfred A. Knopf, 1981.

Fraser, Ronald, ed. *1968: A Student Generation in Revolt/An International Oral History.* New York: Pantheon Books, 1988.

Friedman, Myra. *Buried Alive.* New York: William Morrow, 1973.

Garner, Phillipe. *Contemporary Decorative Arts from 1940 to the Present.* New York: Facts on File, 1980.

Giroud, Françoise. *Christian Dior.* New York: Rizzoli, 1987.

Glynn, Prudence, with Madeleine Ginsburg. *In Fashion: Dress in the Twentieth Century.* New York: Oxford University Press, 1979.

Gottlieb, Annie. *Do You Believe in Magic?.* New York: Times Books, 1987.

Green, John D., and Anthony Haden-Guest. *Birds of Britain.* New York: Macmillan, 1967.

The Guiness Guide to 20th-Century Fashion. London: Guiness Superlatives Ltd., 1981.

Hall-Duncan, Nancy. *The History of Fashion Photography.* New York: Alpine Book Company, 1979.

Haskell, Molly. *From Reverence to Rape: The Treatment of Women in the Movies.* New York: Holt, Rinehart and Winston, 1974.

Hebdige, Dick. *Subculture: The Meaning of Style.* New York: Methuen, Inc., 1979.

Hewison, Robert. *Too Much, Art and Society in the Sixties.* New York: Oxford University Press, 1987.

Hollander, Anne. *Seeing Through Clothes.* New York: Viking Press, 1978.

Horn, Marilyn J. *The Second Skin, An Interdisciplinary Study of Clothing.* New York: Houghton Mifflin Company, 1975.

Horowitz, Gene. *Mr. Jack and the Greenstalks*. New York: W. W. Norton, 1970.

Horowitz, Helen Lefkowitz. *Campus Life*. New York: Alfred A. Knopf, 1987.

Howell, Georgina. *In Vogue*. New York: Schocken Books, 1975.

Hulanicki, Barbara. *From A to Biba*. London: Hutchinson, 1983.

Javna, John and Gordon. *60s!*. New York: St. Martin's Press, 1988.

Jones, Mablen. *Getting It On: The Clothing of Rock 'n' Roll*. New York: Abbeville Press, 1987.

Kaiser, Charles. *1968 in America*. New York: Weidenfeld & Nicholson, 1988.

Keenan, Brigid. *The Women We Wanted to Look Like*. New York: St. Martin's Press, 1977.

Kelly, Katie. *The Wonderful World of Women's Wear Daily*. New York: Saturday Review Press, 1972.

Kennett, Frances. *Secrets of the Couturiers*. London: Orbis, 1985.

Lahr, John. *Automatic Vaudeville: Essays on Star Turns*. London: Heinemann, 1984.

Lakoff, Robin Tolmach, and Scherr, Raquel L. *Face Value: The Politics of Beauty*. Boston: Routlege & Kegan Paul, 1984.

Langner Lawrence. *The Importance of Wearing Clothes*. New York: Hastings House Publishers, 1959.

Law, Lisa. *Flashing on the Sixties*. San Francisco: Chronicle Books, 1988.

Lee, Sarah Tomerlin, ed. *American Fashion: The Lives and Lines of Adrian, Mainbocher, McCardell, Norell, Trigere*. New York: Quadrangle, 1975.

Leigh, Dorien, with Laura Hobe. *The Girl Who Had Everything*. New York: Doubleday, 1980.

Lencek, Lena, and Gideon Bosker. *Making Waves: Swimsuits and the Undressing of America*. San Francisco: Chronicle Books, 1989.

Lichfield, Patrick. *The Most Beautiful Women*. New York: Crescent Books, 1981.

Lurie, Alison. *The Language of Clothes*. New York: Vintage Books, 1981.

Lyman, Ruth, ed. *Couture: An Illustrated History of the Great Paris Designers and Their Creations*. New York: Doubleday and Co., 1972.

Madsen, Axel. *Living for Design: The Yves St. Laurent Story*. New York: Delacourt, 1979.

Makower, Joel. *Boom! Talkin' About Our Generation*. Chicago: A Tilden Press Book/Contemporary Books, Inc., 1985.

Marin, Peter. Photographs by Andes Holmquist. *The Free People*. New York: Outerbridge & Dienstfry, 1969.

Marshall, Beverly. *Smocks and Smocking*. New York: Van Nostrand Reinhold Co., 1981.

Melinkoff, Ellin. *What We Wore: An Offbeat Social History of Women's Clothing, 1950–1980*. New York: Quill, 1984.

Melly, George. *Revolt into Style*. London: Allen Lane, 1970.

Milbank, Caroline Rennolds. *Couture*. New York: Stewart, Tabori & Chang, 1985.

————. *New York Fashion: The Evolution of American Style*. New York: Harry N. Abrams, 1989.

Milinaire, Caterine, and Carol Troy. *Cheap Chic*. New York: Harmony Books, 1975.

Morris, Bernadine. Photographs by Barbara Walz. *The Fashion Makers*. New York: Random House, 1978.

Mulvagh, Jane. *Costume Jewelry in Vogue*. New York: Thames and Hudson, 1988.

————. *Vogue History of 20th Century Fashion*. New York: Viking, 1989.

Obst, Linda Rosen, ed. *The Sixties*. New York: Random House/Rolling Stone Press, 1977.

O'Hara, Georgina. *The Encyclopedia of Fashion*. New York: Harry N. Abrams, 1986.

O'Neill, William. *Coming Apart*. New York: Quadrangle Books, 1971.

Parker, Rozsika. *The Subversive Stitch: Embroidery and the Making of the Feminine*. New York: Routledge, 1989.

Peck, Abe. *Uncovering the Sixties: The Life & Times of the Underground Press*. New York: Pantheon Books, 1985.

Perry, Charles. *The Haight-Ashbury: A History*. New York: Random House/Rolling Stone Press, 1984.

Phillips, John, with Jim Jerome. *Papa John*. New York: Doubleday, 1986.

Phillips, Michelle. *California Dreamin'*. New York: Warner Books, 1986.

Picken, Mary Brooks. *The Fashion Dictionary*. New York: Funk & Wagnalls, 1973.

Pierre, Clara. *Looking Good*. New York: Reader's Digest Press, 1976.

Powell, Polly, and Lucy Peel. *'50s & '60s Style*. Secaucus, New Jersey: Chartwell Books, Inc., 1988.

Quant, Mary. *Quant on Quant*. London: Cassel & Co, 1966.

Reich, Charles. *The Greening of America: How the Youth Revolution Is Trying to Make America Livable*. New York: Random House, 1970.

Rhodes, Zandra, and Anne Knight. *The Art of Zandra Rhodes*. Boston: Houghton Mifflin Co., 1984.

Roach, Mary Ellen, and Joanne Bubolz Eicher, eds. *Dress, Adornment and the Social Order*. New York: John Wiley & Sons, Inc., 1965.

Roscho, Bernard. *The Rag Race*. New York: Funk & Wagnalls Company, Inc., 1963.

Rosen, Marjorie. *Popcorn Venus: Women, Movies & the American Dream*. New York: Coward, McCann & Geoghegan, 1973.

Rudofsky, Bernard. *The Unfashionable Human Body*. New York: Doubleday, 1971.

Sandler, Irving. *American Art of the 1960s*. New York: Harper & Row, 1988.

Sassoon, Vidal. *Sorry I Kept You Waiting, Madam*. New York: G. P. Putnam's Sons, 1968.

Scaduto, Anthony. *Mick Jagger*. New York: David McKay Company, Inc., 1974.

Schreier, Barbara. *Mystique and Identity: Women's Fashions of the 1950's*. Norfolk, Virginia: The Chrysler Museum, 1984.

Shields, Jody. *All That Glitters: The Glory of Costume Jewelry*. London, Boston, Sydney: Rizzoli, 1987.

Shots of Style. London: Victoria and Albert Museum, 1985.

Shrimpton, Jean. *My Own Story: The Truth About Modelling*. New York: Bantam, 1965.

Silverman, Debora. *Selling Culture*. New York: Pantheon Books, 1986.

Sims, Naomi. *How to Be a Top Model*. New York: Doubleday, 1979.

Somma, Robert, ed. *No One Waved Good-Bye*. New York: Outerbridge & Deinstfry, 1971.

Steele, Valerie. *Fashion and Eroticism: Ideals of Feminine Beauty from the Victorian Era to the Jazz Age*. New York: Oxford University Press, 1985.

————. *Paris Fashion*. New York: Oxford University Press, 1988.

Stegemeyer, Anne. *Who's Who in Fashion*. New York: Fairchild Publications, 1980.

Stein, Jean, and George Plimpton. *Edie*. New York: Alfred A. Knopf, 1982.

Taylor, Derek. *It Was Twenty Years Ago Today*. New York: Simon & Schuster/A Fireside Book, 1987.

Time Annual. *1969: The Year in Review*. New York: Time-Life Books, 1970.

Tompkins, Calvin. *Off the Wall: Robert Rauschenberg and the Art World of Our Time*. New York: Doubleday, 1980.

Trasko, Mary. *Heavenly Soles: Extraordinary Twentieth-Century Shoes*. New York: Abbeville Press, 1989.

Twiggy. *Twiggy, An Autobiography*. London: Mayflower Books, 1976.

Unger, Irwin, and Debi Unger. *Turning Point: 1968*. New York: Charles Scribner's Sons, 1988.

Vecchio, Robert. *The Fashion Makers/A Photographic Record*. Text by Robert Riley. New York: Crown, 1967.

Walker, Alexander. *Hollywood U.K.* New York: Stein & Day, 1974.

Warhol, Andy, with Pat Hackett. *Popism: The Warhol Sixties*. New York: Harcourt, Brace, Jovanovich, 1980.

Wheen, Francis. *The Sixties*. London: Century Publishing, 1982.

Wolfe, Tom. *The Kandy-Kolored Tangerine-Flake Streamline Baby*. New York: Farrar, Straus & Giroux, 1965.

————. *The Pump House Gang*. New York: Farrar, Straus & Giroux, 1968.

————. *Radical Chic and Mau-Mauing the Flak Catchers*. New York: Farrar, Straus & Giroux, 1970.

Young, Jean, and Michael Lang. *Woodstock Festival Remembered*. New York: Ballantine Books, 1979.

ACKNOWLEDGMENTS

I wish to thank the subjects interviewed for this book, many of whom contributed not only their memories but helped in locating additional sources: Benedetta Barzini, Nally Bellati, Joan Juliet Buck, Michael Chow, Dory Coffee, Carol Friedland Cohen, Jean Shrimpton Cox, Pilar Crespi, Winkie Donovan, Joe Eula, Duggie Fields, Michael Fish, Stephen Fitz-Simon, Marion Foale, Jo and Ulrich Franzen, Myra Friedman, Linda Gravenites, Felicity Green, Lauren Greene, Anthony Haden-Guest, Colette Mimram Haron, Holly Harp, Stan Herman, Barbara Hulanicki, Betsey Johnson, Kezia Keeble, the late Mrs. Frederick (Sally) Kirkland, the late John Kloss, Vernon Lambert, Deanna Littell, Richard Maher, Ingeborg Marcus, Caterine Milinaire, Peggy Moffitt, Michael Mott, Pat Nichols, the late Maning Obregon, Anita Pallenberg, Mary Peacock, Sara Penn, Patricia Peterson, Father Bradley Pierce, Mary Quant, O.B.E., Jane Rainey, Zandra Rhodes, Bob Rogers, Joan Sibley Powell, Ethel Scull, Chelita Secunda, Elena Solow, Francis Patiky Stein, Elisa Stone, Sally Tuffin, Nigel Waymouth, James Wedge, Susannah York, Paul Young.

I would like to thank the photographers who researched their files (please see the photo credits following the index) and the administrative personnel who graciously handled my requests: Shelley Dowell at Richard Avedon, Debra Cohen, Arnold Horton and Rebecca Victor at the *Life Magazine* picture service, Sally at Gosta Peterson's studio, Lynn Bowe at Magnum Photos, Claudine at French *Elle,* Gene Keesee at Photo Trends, Sandra Brind and Charlotte Brown at the London *Sunday Times,* Gil Curry at Zandra Rhodes, Ltd., Chris at Baron Wolman's studio, Barry Ratoff at Charles Tracy Studio, Louise Bonnett at Mary Quant.

My parents are a bedrock of encouragement. I am grateful for the advice given by Bruce Boyce, Lucille Krasne, Francis Mason, Elena Tchernichova, and the personal support from the members of Nichiren Shoshu of America. I owe an enormous debt of gratitude to my agent, Joan Brookbank. At Abbeville Press, my editor, Alan Axelrod, and the company's art director, Renée Khatami, lent superb guidance to this project. I want to thank Abbeville's president, Robert E. Abrams, for his belief in this book.

INDEX

Page numbers in *italics* refer to illustrations and captions.